Library Transformation Strategies

Series Editor
Fabrice Papy

Library Transformation Strategies

Jean-Philippe Accart

WILEY

First published 2022 in Great Britain and the United States by ISTE Ltd and John Wiley & Sons, Inc.

Apart from any fair dealing for the purposes of research or private study, or criticism or review, as permitted under the Copyright, Designs and Patents Act 1988, this publication may only be reproduced, stored or transmitted, in any form or by any means, with the prior permission in writing of the publishers, or in the case of reprographic reproduction in accordance with the terms and licenses issued by the CLA. Enquiries concerning reproduction outside these terms should be sent to the publishers at the undermentioned address:

ISTE Ltd
27-37 St George's Road
London SW19 4EU
UK

www.iste.co.uk

John Wiley & Sons, Inc.
111 River Street
Hoboken, NJ 07030
USA

www.wiley.com

© ISTE Ltd 2022

The rights of Jean-Philippe Accart to be identified as the author of this work have been asserted by him in accordance with the Copyright, Designs and Patents Act 1988.

Any opinions, findings, and conclusions or recommendations expressed in this material are those of the author(s), contributor(s) or editor(s) and do not necessarily reflect the views of ISTE Group.

Library of Congress Control Number: 2022941222

British Library Cataloguing-in-Publication Data
A CIP record for this book is available from the British Library
ISBN 978-1-78630-887-0

Contents

Foreword. ix

Introduction. xiii

Part 1. The Environment and Society 1

Chapter 1. Societal Changes and Libraries 3

    1.1. In terms of innovation 3
    1.2. In the working world. 4
    1.3. In the world of professional associations 7

Chapter 2. Economic Changes. 9

    2.1. An evolving documentary and information activity. 9
    2.2. The information economy. 10
        2.2.1. Some figures 10
        2.2.2. Free information 11
        2.2.3. An economic approach to information and libraries 13
    2.3. Information as a public asset 15
        2.3.1. Free of charge, information and public libraries 16
        2.3.2. Why pay for information? 17
    2.4. The Internet and digital technology 19
    2.5. Towards new economic models 20
    2.6. The theory of knowledge commons 20

Chapter 3. The Evolution of the Library Space — 23

3.1. From the perspective of creation and innovation — 23
3.2. From the third place to DIY — 24
    3.2.1. Digital public spaces (Espaces Publics Numériques, EPN) in France — 26
    3.2.2. Some examples of Fab Labs in American libraries — 28
3.3. Learning spaces or learning centers — 28
3.4. The Smart Libraries concept — 29
3.5. Wellness spaces — 31
3.6. Reception areas: a user-oriented approach — 33
3.7. The use of the library space — 35
3.8. Green libraries — 37

Chapter 4. Legal Changes — 39

4.1. GDPR: European data protection regulations, as applied to libraries — 39
    4.1.1. The fields of application — 40
    4.1.2. Data processing and hosting — 41
4.2. Protection of personal data — 42

Part 2. Human Resources and Management — 45

Chapter 5. New Management Theories Applicable to Libraries — 47

5.1. Participatory management — 48
    5.1.1. The five principles of participatory management — 48
    5.1.2. The qualities required for participatory management — 49
5.2. Management by benevolence or well-treatment — 50
5.3. Empathy, a management method? — 52
5.4. Change management (CM) — 53
    5.4.1. The three levels of change management — 55
5.5. Project management: theory and applications — 55
    5.5.1. Project mode operation: two case studies — 56

Chapter 6. Some Theory on Management and Leadership — 65

6.1. New management methods: Design Thinking, user experience and agile methods — 66
    6.1.1. Design Thinking — 67
    6.1.2. User experience (UX) — 69
6.2. User power — 71

6.3. Setting up and managing an agile project.	72
6.3.1. The application of agile methods	73
6.3.2. Agility in libraries	74
6.4. Library management and leadership, constantly redefined concepts	75

Part 3. Library Tools and Technology. 77

Chapter 7. The Digital Transformation of Libraries 79

7.1. The library as a service: from catalogues to digital platforms. .	80
7.1.1. Service platforms	80
7.1.2. Library intranets, information portals and digital repositories	85
7.1.3. Monitoring, business intelligence and curation platforms. .	88
7.1.4. Social platforms	91
7.2. Digital archiving of documents.	95
7.2.1. Document archiving: an overview of open access	96
7.2.2. Dissemination methods	98
7.2.3. European Open Access Policy.	100

Chapter 8. Other Technologies for Library Transformation 103

8.1. Blockchain.	103
8.2. Augmented/virtual reality in libraries	104
8.2.1. A brief history of augmented reality	105
8.2.2. Augmented reality explained.	106
8.3. Artificial intelligence (AI) and robotics.	106

Part 4. Marketing 109

Chapter 9. Marketing Dimensions in Libraries. 111

9.1. Digital marketing.	111
9.2. The user at the heart of transformation	112
9.2.1. Addressing ongoing challenges	112
9.2.2. Capturing the user's attention online	113
9.3. Adopting a five-step marketing approach.	115
9.4. Everyday marketing	118

Chapter 10. The User at the Heart: Mediation — 121

10.1. Keeping in touch with the user: mediation — 122
10.2. Mediation(s) — 124
    10.2.1. Library mediation — 125
    10.2.2. Social mediation — 126
    10.2.3. Cultural mediation — 127
    10.2.4. Digital mediation — 127
    10.2.5. Scientific mediation — 128

Chapter 11. The Library's Digital Identity — 131

11.1. Defining identity — 131
11.2. From the individual to the group and the library institution — 133
11.3. Profiles, behavior and traces on the Internet — 135

Chapter 12. Adopting a Library Branding Strategy — 139

12.1. Defining the brand concept — 140
12.2. Brands and libraries — 141
12.3. The brand world — 143

Conclusion — 147

References — 149

Index — 153

Foreword

Libraries need to be kitchens, active social places where you mix a rich set of ingredients (information, resources, talents) into an exciting new concoction that can then be shared[1].

R.D. Lankes

Throughout his book/advocacy, R.D. Lankes encourages audiences to demand excellent libraries, which they deserve, because:

The library is part of the community. It is not a set of comfy chairs and an excellent collection. It is a symbol, and a friend, and a teacher[2].

However, a simple wave of a magic wand is not enough to convert them into (gastronomic) kitchens, to make them our (precious) allies and (inspiring) trainers! It is necessary to set up and develop real strategies in order to achieve a general transformation, without which information services of all kinds will not survive.

---

1 Lankes, R.D. (2018). Demanding better libraries for today's complex world: Advocacy for a new library economy, 97 [Online]. Available at: http://ateliers.sens-public.org/exigeons-de-meilleures-bibliotheques/index.html [Accessed November 10, 2019].
2 *Ibid.*, p. 228.

In fact, in a 2016 interview, the director of Switzerland's largest scientific library, the *École Polytechnique Fédérale de Zurich*, said:

> Until now, libraries have only collected information for people. That concept doesn't work nowadays. There is the internet. Whoever is looking for content doesn't need libraries anymore[3].

He caused an uproar, (ab)used a cliché and expressed himself very clumsily, but he nevertheless raised the very real question of the future of libraries, the challenges and issues they face, the changes they must make and the resulting adaptations to the role of the librarian. Unfortunately, this was without any constructive spirit, without really proposing any avenues of reflection or with a view to putting transformation at the heart of existing projects in progress.

Fortunately, Jean-Philippe Accart is here to encourage us to pursue the transformation of our libraries, no matter how big or small the transformation. In this 18th book, the renowned author shows us how information services have been trying to reform themselves for several years in order to adapt to their rapidly changing environment. Society is changing, access to information and research habits are evolving and the public is using libraries differently. Consequently, their survival depends on their adaptation to new uses, through the implementation of what he calls "steering and transformation strategies".

The concepts of the "third place library" and its natural extension, the "four spaces model"[4], devised in 2012 by three Danish information sciences professors, have been discussed and applied, here and there, for several years. While these are fundamental models that contribute to the profound evolution of our libraries, they must be part of a more general strategy to develop their full impact.

---

3 Ball, R. (2016). *Neue Zürcher Zeitung am Sonntag*. Translation from German.

4 Beudon, N. (2019). Les quatre dimensions des bibliothèques. Le recueil factice : un blog qui parle de [...] [Online]. Available at: http://lrf-blog.com/2019/07/03/les-quatre-dimensions-des-bibliotheques/ [Accessed November 10, 2019].

Jean-Philippe Accart's proposal is to present a number of strategies and interesting real-life experiences, paths to be followed by librarians who have understood the issues and are determined to evolve: from the renewal of the library space to the library as a service and the archiving of data in the Cloud, as well as numerous notions on management and marketing, as they apply to our libraries.

It is possible to ensure a promising future for librarians, by making them "excellent", in accordance with what their audiences have the right to demand, following the vision of R.D. Lankes, whose ambition I share. However, the future depends entirely on the willingness and ability of staff to take charge of their institutions, as he states just as clearly:

> … Without excellent librarians, it is impossible to have excellent libraries[5].

Consequently, librarians must urgently develop or acquire interpersonal and teaching skills in communication, marketing and cultural and digital mediation, as well as in management and administration. This is the only way that transformation strategies will really bear fruit.

Good training (basic and continuous) of staff is therefore the driving force behind current and future changes. Fear of change is always lurking in the wings and can slow down the evolution towards information services that are adapted to the needs of their audiences and resolutely forward-looking.

Jean-Philippe Accart eloquently contributes to our training and accompanies us in these necessary changes, by being both convincing and reassuring. For my part, I am trying to help train critical librarians, capable of transforming our libraries. Together, we

---

5 Lankes, R.D. (2018). Demanding better libraries for today's complex world: Advocacy for a new library economy, 97, 216 [Online]. Available at: http://ateliers.sens-public.org/demand-better-libraries/index.html [Accessed November 10, 2019].

have the will to contribute to the success of the library model of tomorrow.

Michel GORIN
Senior lecturer HES
Documentary Information Department
Geneva School of Business Administration
Switzerland

Introduction

I.1. Transformation at the heart of library projects

The aim of this book is to present the different ways in which libraries and information services are transforming – or are in the process of transforming – in order to adapt to the current world, to move forward and to anticipate various trends or movements. It should be noted that this transformation movement is not recent, but dates back several years, is gathering pace and forcibly affecting traditional knowledge structures, namely libraries and information services in general.

These structures are adopting, implementing and developing management and transformation strategies that are having major repercussions on the lives of institutions or services, employees and collaborators and on the public. The traditional rules of management, even if they still apply, are gradually changing. These changes are manifold and can be seen as lacking unity or meaning in relation to the roles attributed to libraries: running video or photo workshops, lending tools or costumes or setting up a "Fab Lab"[1] seem far removed from their original missions. Why do libraries embark on such experiments, which may seem risky, but are successful in many

---

[1] A Fab Lab (a short form of the term Fabrication Laboratory) is a place open to the public where all kinds of tools, including computer-controlled machine tools, are made available for designing and producing objects. Definition: Carrefour de l'innovation, May 2019.

cases? Should the new library be seen as a platform for multiple and diverse services, whether digital or on site?

It goes without saying that the strategies described here cannot all be undertaken simultaneously: the aim is to bring them together in a coherent manner, with a view to drawing up a picture of the current situation, as well as to provide guidelines for professionals who wish to develop their structures. A very positive point for libraries is the new projects (architectural, service, managerial and so on) that abound and are only waiting to be taken up and adapted.

Although numerous transformation strategies are described here, this book does not claim to list them all or to be exhaustive. The most recent experiences, those that appear to be representative or innovative, are included here and developed. There are certainly others that are just as interesting and exemplary.

After the theme of change, which has been well used, the theme of library "transformation" is representative and appropriate for our time; it appears to be the current *leitmotif* for the professional world and was chosen as the generic theme of the 2018 World Library and Information Conference (WLIC-IFLA)[2]. We might even be tempted to say, without straying too far from reality, that without transformation no salvation will be possible. It would indeed be very risky to ignore major movements that feed our society, including certain categories of the population (such as young people and seniors), and that are leading to a transformation of society in general: for example, digital technology is generating many changes in behavior with regard to information, information transfer and understanding of information, a subject to which we will return. However, the societal transformations discussed in Part 1 affect the entire population, not just young people or seniors. One of the missions – and strengths – of libraries is specifically transversality, in other words, their applicability to all publics, whatever they are, without distinction. This is one of the aspects that this book focuses on.

---

2 Available at: https://2018.ifla.org/: the theme of the conference was "Transform libraries, Transform societies".

I.2. How to use this book

This book is divided into four parts, illustrating how library management and transformation strategies interact with each other and create momentum.

Part 1, "The Environment and Society", demonstrates that the many organizational changes affecting the world of work (private and public sectors) are clearly also influencing knowledge institutions, with significant consequences for library work. Furthermore, the library environment is changing, with a reconfiguration of space that allows for innovation and creation to become a space of well-being.

Part 2, "Human Resources and Management", introduces several management concepts that are, or will be, applied in knowledge institutions:

– participatory management;

– management by benevolence or good treatment;

– management by empathy;

– management by projects;

– change management.

Hierarchical, top-down forms of management still exist, especially in larger institutions, but small- and medium-sized teams can apply more flexible and participative methods. Using project management and agile methods in the library, it is possible to introduce change to teams, involving them more in ongoing projects. New project approaches, such as Design Thinking or User Experience, are linked to Chapter 5. Part 2 closes with the implementation and management of an agile project.

Part 3, "Library Tools and Technology", is essential for understanding current issues in libraries and documentation services: adaptations have been constant for several decades, but are even more so today. Digital (documentary, monitoring or social) platforms have become essential and integrate many services. Other technological aspects have an influence, such as virtual reality, artificial intelligence, blockchain and robotics.

Part 4, "Marketing", puts the user at the heart of the action and of the documentary activity. To do this, information mediation, detailed in all its implications, is necessary. Marketing theories applied to libraries make them more visible to the public, decision-makers and funders. This visibility is also achieved through a brand strategy.

PART 1

The Environment and Society

1
Societal Changes and Libraries

1.1. In terms of innovation

Whatever the field of activity – public reading, university library, scientific library, documentation, information or even archive service – innovation is everywhere and is inseparable from the evolution that has always taken place within libraries. It should be pointed out here that innovation is not only technological, but also refers to ways of working or managing relationships and human resources. Some examples:

– the purchase of a new library management system;

– the adoption of different rules, norms and working standards (cataloging, indexing, referencing, classification and so on);

– subscribing to suppliers who offer better benefits for access to, for example, information resources.

There are also many examples of changes and developments:

– in terms of documentary services, the introduction of new services entails changes in various areas: procedures, regulations and techniques all have to be modified;

– on the administrative level, an alternative hierarchy, with new missions and including a different organization chart from that of the establishment or service, can constitute important innovation factors, as well as presenting the composition of a team modified following departures, resignations and illnesses: the recruitment of an innovative profile – or one oriented towards innovative practices – changes the dynamics within a team;

– beyond the institution itself, the cultural, political and economic context has a definite impact;

– the same applies to changes in regulations and legal provisions, such as copyrights and patents and the European General Data Protection Regulation (GDPR).

This does not even take into account public behaviors with regard to their varied use of information services, which will have to be adapted.

Whether these innovations are structural or functional, they are having a significant impact on work and its organization, on the identification of staff with their establishment or work structure, on their general involvement and on the service provided to the public.

No innovation is without risk, but it is necessary to the life of the organization and should even become an inherent part of it. It is not that the organization has to innovate all the time, but innovation should be a state of mind. Some organizations have innovation cells or departments that depend on R&D to develop new concepts and products that are then adopted by their customers: it is not so different in the information science fields, although the methods are more informal and may rely on a few innovative professionals. The rules for design and marketing need to be clear and easily understood, an example being the rules around the introduction of new document services.

1.2. In the working world

Although the activity of libraries and information services is directly linked to the economy, as are other cultural sectors, in France it is mostly dependent on public funds and taxes levied on the population. This activity is difficult to justify to private decision-makers, financiers or elected representatives in terms of returns, profits or benefits, at least on a purely material level. It always remains somewhat hidden or in the background. It is, however, valuable in other ways, since, in the eyes of information professionals, the benefits are clear:

– that an economy of scale in terms of documentary resources is possible: when these are centralized from multiple sites, they are better managed;

– this avoids their dispersion for a more efficient result;

– this leads to a better knowledge and use of these resources;

– it allows for significant gains to be accrued from the management – especially financial – of information;

– it plays a part in the continuous training of personnel within a company or institution.

However, in the current economic climate, some private companies and public institutions are cutting back on budgets, services and human resources. Libraries and information services are the first to suffer from these budgetary restrictions, which are disappearing or being drastically reduced. A number of French cities and departments are even closing their public libraries. Others are reducing their opening hours, while the public demand is for hours to be extended. We will see that there are solutions to counter movements such as these that do not meet the needs of the public.

In organizations, the changes are political and managerial, but they are linked to socioeconomic reasons. Increasingly, corporate governance views the information–documentation function differently and uses a number of reductive arguments, such as:

– this can easily be replaced by a fully digital solution;

– the function is integrated into infrastructure services, IT departments or marketing communications;

– the function can also be diluted among a group of people (employees, managers, secretaries). The question of information mediation – and digital mediation in particular – is then posed with acuity, as it is not or no longer fulfilled[1].

There is a risk that companies or institutions will find themselves in the same situation as before (1970–1980s), where the information–documentation function was very poorly developed and where each employee was left to their own devices in relation to the information they had to find, select, analyze and synthesize, etc. There is a real risk of losing information or of taking for granted erroneous, false or fraudulent information that has not been evaluated and validated by professionals. According to the *Association Information et Management* (AIM)[2], an employee spends an average of 7.5 hours a week looking for information, whether on paper or in digital form, without finding it[3].

These changes in organizations lead to the use of alternative solutions to manage and retrieve useful information. The independent activity can then find its place, because the information professionals are able to propose:

– individualized services, *à la carte*, allowing a certain versatility and flexibility, which can be internalized or outsourced;

– one-off services that can be budgeted for in advance by companies.

This encourages part-time work or telecommuting.

Policy makers, financiers and business managers do not, on the whole, have an accurate perception of the information–documentation profession – they often limit their thinking to the "books" aspect (or to print in general), which is a small part of the overall documentary activity. Some European countries have seen public library budgets drastically reduced, as in Great Britain, where several hundred libraries have been closed in recent years (441 in 2016, out of a

---

1 See Part 4, "Marketing".
2 https://www.facebook.com/Association.Information.Management.AIM/.
3 https://digital-solutions.konicaminolta.fr/combien-de-temps-perdez-vous-a-chercher-un-document/, accessed July 23, 2019.

network of 4,500 libraries[4]). Others are putting people with no particular skills in this function at the head of public institutions, notably in certain international organizations or municipalities that recruit administrators[5].

The reason often given (apart from political reasons), which is also based on a false idea of the profession, is that it is difficult to recruit experienced professionals, whereas more than 1,500 students graduate from the 100 existing training courses run in France every year and have been doing so for many years[6]... This truly raises the issue of the public perception of the profession and its visibility in general.

It is clear that information professionals have a role to play in addressing the information deficit within organizations and even among the general public. The search for accurate and relevant information is the responsibility of trained and competent professionals.

1.3. In the world of professional associations

The world of professional associations, while innovative in the 1980s through the 2000s, is now suffering the full force of the budgetary and staffing restrictions described above: documentalists and librarians no longer join or participate in training courses or organized activities because of a lack of budget or time, or because they are not authorized to participate by their superiors. Professionals also lack the time to volunteer and there is a significant decline in the role of associations representing the information professions.

---

4 http://www.archimag.com/bibliotheque-edition/2016/02/18/grande-bretagne-441-biblioth%C3%A8ques-ferm%C3%A9es-cause-aust%C3%A9rit%C3%A9, accessed July 23, 2019.
5 This was the case at the Bibliothèque Alcazar in Marseille.
6 Figures cited – all degrees combined – in: Accart, J.-P. (2015). *Le Métier de documentaliste*. Éditions du Cercle de la Librairie, Paris.

The situation is, of course, different in each country[7]:

– at present, in France, the *Association des Bibliothécaires de France* (ABF) is doing well compared to the *Association des Professionnels de l'Information et de la Documentation* (known by the initials ADBS), which is relatively weak. It is a pity that national or local professional associations do not come together in an umbrella organization that can represent and defend them. There is, of course, a plethora of other associations besides the ABF, for music, for university library directors and for archivists;

– at the European level, LIBER (*Ligue des Bibliothèques Européennes de Recherche* – Association of European Research Libraries), which brings together professionals from study and research libraries, is as dynamic as the European Association for Health Information and Libraries, EAHIL.

The International Federation of Library Associations (IFLA) has succeeded in having libraries included in the United Nations 2030 Agenda and is engaged in numerous lobbying activities with governments and decision-makers. The Federation now has 1,500 institutional members (national associations and institutions) in over 150 countries[8]. Lobbying is also an individual matter that every professional must integrate into their daily activities.

---

7 ABF: https://www.abf.asso.fr/; ADBS: https://www.adbs.fr/; LIBER: https://libereurope.eu/; IFLA: http://www.ifla.org.
8 2019 figures provided during the IFLA Annual Conference in Athens, August 2019.

2

Economic Changes

2.1. An evolving documentary and information activity

Based on the reasons given in the previous chapter, which are only some of the reasons stated, certain consequences ensue for the organization of the work in libraries and information services:

– with fewer staff recruited or reduced opening hours, tasks are reorganized and existing staff become multiskilled. This is not a recent phenomenon, as documentation services often operate with only a few staff, who carry out multiple tasks and work. In France, these comprise between one and five professionals and are therefore small- and medium-sized services. Libraries operate differently, with each staff member being assigned a specific task, but often the circulation service is shared between members of the same team;

– as we have seen, if the information function within an organization disappears or is dramatically reduced, it is then entrusted to non-professionals. They obviously cannot perform the same tasks, nor offer the same quality of service. The function is therefore not completely fulfilled, which leads to a loss of information and less dissemination;

– the company or institution can call on subcontractors, outsourcing and entrusting documentary tasks to external consultants who are paid for their services: this is the case for certain information activities, such as press reviews, occasional or systematic information searches or updating of web pages. This solution makes it possible to fulfil a deficient information function;

– some organizations are going all-digital and eliminating paper documentation, with a view to moving towards zero paper. Even while this solution is interesting and we are moving towards a digital society, access to information is not so easy for all those wishing to consult it, to extract what is relevant and can be used in their daily work or in their private and social lives and which is often still based on paper or print. Full digitization of all printed publications is still far away and the digital divide for all generations is also far from being bridged[1].

2.2. The information economy

2.2.1. *Some figures*

At this point, it is important to give some figures – from journal subscriptions and the online database market – that reveal the current information economy:

– libraries and information services have been heavily impacted for many years by increases in journal and database subscription prices, dictated by international publishers. The above factors make it even more difficult for libraries and information services to manage their budgets. Prices are effectively increasing by 18% for general information products, compared with 10% increases in database subscriptions, 36% for electronic periodicals and 75% for e-books. On average, the annual increase for a subscription is between 2 and 5%[2];

---

1 The digital divide most often refers to the inequality of access to digital technologies (mainly computers) and sometimes to the divide between "infotransmitters and inforeceivers". This inequality is strongly marked between the developed countries of the West and the countries of the South, known as developing countries. See https://www.techno-science.net/definition/3957.html.

2 Figures given at the Consortium of Swiss Academic Libraries annual conference, June 2019.

– in addition to this regular increase, there is the value-added tax (VAT), which varies according to the information media: for e-books, it is 2.5%, and for databases 7.5%.

How do we respond? Many libraries are cutting back on subscriptions or e-book purchases or negotiating with publishers on a case-by-case basis. Some are refusing to accept these increases and are cancelling subscriptions altogether. Others – especially in the academic world – are choosing to pool resources and form consortia, like the Couperin Consortium in France or the Swiss Consortium of Academic Libraries[3]. Another approach is open access, which is discussed in Part 3.

The public's perception of free information is therefore false or distorted by the fact that a certain type of information freely circulates and is accessible to all. For professional information (contained in databases), on the other hand, it has to be acquired through commercial intermediaries, the Information Providers. The situation is more complex and needs to be analyzed.

2.2.2. Free information

The last 20 years have seen major technological changes in how information is accessed, which have themselves led to other behaviors in relation to this same information. The paradox is not any less between, on the one hand, a society based on market relations and therefore on money and, on the other hand, the illusion that with information at hand (or at our fingertips, or even based on voice or facial recognition), nothing is easier to obtain for free. In order to understand the issues of free/paid access, it is first necessary to consider information and libraries through the prism of economics, then to consider information as a public asset, which is what several economists advocate; secondly, to see what the question of free access to libraries and paid information really means. In conclusion,

---

3 Supervised by the Swiss Library Network for Education and Research (SLiNER) and integrated into the Swiss Library Service Platform (SLSP).

information available digitally and online is accelerating the development of economic models.

Does it not give a distorted picture of the real situation to make people believe – especially the younger generations – that everything is free on digital information networks? What about copyright, among other things? Clearly, we are not calling into question the information networks, as they exist and are currently developing. On the contrary, it is simply worth recalling a few elements that even some professionals seem to have forgotten, dedicated as they are to the very laudable fight for generally free information. This type of struggle raises many questions about what should be free (or considered free) and what should be paid for: the image of libraries and librarians is itself affected, as users do not understand why such and such a service is paid for (access to the Internet, for example) when it is found within a public service. Since our profession is already struggling to be truly recognized (it is often associated with volunteering or with a profession for which no diploma is necessary, or that can be achieved for free), is offering free services the best way to change this perception (something being free being often associated with the lack of value)?

Changing the subject from that of public libraries, documentation services have been debating for many years about the added value of the information services they offer, which is real, as information has become an economic asset. What is their argument? What is the reason for this difference between the public sector, where we find the majority of libraries, and the private sector, where the information function is carried out? Should we see this as a conceptual difference regarding access to information through the free/paid prism?

What do the theorists of the information economy, who see information as an economic rather than a cultural asset, tell us? How does public reading fit in with all of this?

2.2.3. *An economic approach to information and libraries*

In recent years, economics has resolutely entered the world of libraries: to give a striking example, many current projects for the restructuring of university libraries resemble corporate projects, advancing hitherto little-used concepts such as profitability, downsizing and regular task evaluation. Libraries no longer appear to be the sustainable entities they once were; the economic crisis has seen to that, as demonstrated by the recent Anglo-Saxon and Canadian examples. The situation in France is somewhat different, except for certain company documentation services, which are penalized and simply disappear, because they are deemed unprofitable.

For public libraries, the situation appears to be more stable in France than in the countries quoted above. An economic approach to information is making it possible to highlight the issues related to information, three of which can be defined:

– strategic: a company or institution, in order to thrive and survive, must know its partners and competitors at the local, national and international levels; libraries have understood this well by developing networks and consortia and have done so for decades; documentation services keep a close watch on the company's environment;

– economic: the information sector constitutes a reserve of services and therefore jobs; new roles are being created such as community manager, records manager, knowledge manager and web manager; more traditional roles (librarian, documentalist, archivist) are converging while activities complement each other, such as museums and libraries or documentation services, or archives and libraries;

– cultural: information is not neutral. This is evidenced by the concentration of English and German scientific and technical information in the hands of a few large publishers (such as Elsevier and Springer). Culture and the economy are closely intertwined, with the economy increasingly predominant.

At present, the information market corresponds to a logic of supply and demand. According to Austrian economist Fritz Machlup, the information economy covers a complex field of concepts and intentions to:

– optimize the communication system;

– analyze the cost–benefit ratio;

– merge decision theory, operational research and team theory.

Thus, several types of information can be distinguished:

– resource information: generally considered to be free;

– stock information: refers to memory and heritage. It is constantly transformed thanks to new technologies;

– information flow: allows exchange thanks to standards (such as SGML and XML);

– product information: becomes a product thanks to the development of new media;

– service information: from being a product, information becomes a service with the notions of mediation, accompaniment, servuction[4] and advice;

– asset information: when disseminated, the information belongs first to its producer–sender, then to its receiver(s);

– process information: concerns the sender–receiver relationship.

These remarks by Machlup summarize in a relevant and logical way the cycle of information, seen as an asset.

---

4 Neologism constructed from the words "service" and "production". The concept of servuction was developed by Pierre Eiglier and Éric Langeard. It represents all the material and human elements used, as well as the activities deployed to design, create and develop the service that a company wishes to offer to the market, according to a chosen quality level. See https://www.e-marketing.fr/Definitions-Glossaire/Servuction-243127.htm#mEC9OQgkMHYTr0Yt.97.

2.3. Information as a public asset

From a civic and cultural point of view, access to information is seen as a right. Public taxation is often put forward as justification, and rightly so (I pay taxes, therefore...). Public libraries are striving to keep their services free, despite many pressures. Information helps in decision-making and is becoming an economic asset, with added value through its processing. Documentalists therefore feel that it is justified to charge for services, based on the value added from searching, selecting and processing information. In principle, researchers are setting up free circulation of scientific knowledge: the development of open archives is proof of this, but it is often public funds that take over after private investment. Most of the time, it is university librarians who manage open archives, their salaries paid for by the university and therefore from public funds. So, nothing is truly free.

Where do we find funding for private documentation services or public libraries? Any time when equipment, material, premises and know-how costs are increasing, the question is raised. There are various opposing or overlapping arguments, but it is important to set them out:

– in the event of a crisis, documentation services, which take up a significant part of the company's budget, survive only through the application of a fee structure;

– users of the information are also consumers of the service and must bear part of the cost of the service;

– contributions from the application of a tariff by public services remain earmarked for the sole purpose of improving the services in question;

– in the interests of equality, access to information is public and free of charge, since charging creates inequalities.

The pragmatic question of the cost of information is essential at the present time and is posed to all information professionals. It forces us to make choices, sometimes drastic ones.

In France, the question of funding for public libraries has not yet really been raised, unlike in some countries, such as the United States, Canada and the Netherlands. One of the answers provided by librarians is to resort to private patronage, to foundations or individuals willing to finance libraries, or to associations specifically created for services that the library cannot provide alone[5]. In universities and business schools, alumni are called upon to contribute large sums of money. Finding funding justifies the creation of a position dedicated to sponsorship to seek private funds or to create private–public partnerships.

2.3.1. *Free of charge, information and public libraries*

Since their creation during the French Revolution, with the confiscation of clergy and nobility property ("books are placed at the disposal of the Nation"), but especially since the 19th century, French public libraries and librarians have been committed to the principle of free access. No one questions this principle in France, as far as the public service is concerned: a fairly modest registration fee may be charged to citizens by some public libraries and to students by university libraries (usually included in the tuition fees). This registration fee is, moreover, highly symbolic and does not reflect reality regarding the price of the book purchased in a bookshop or the costs incurred by processing it in a library: it does, however, seal a moral contract between the lending institution, the library, the borrower and the patron; the patron undertakes to return the borrowed documents in good condition. The issue of fines (for late, damaged or lost documents) is more difficult to resolve, as it often puts library professionals in a difficult position when faced with recalcitrant patrons for the reimbursement or replacement of damaged or lost documents. However, if the patron refuses to reimburse, they will be banned from borrowing, which is ultimately a way of making them understand that not everything can be free[6].

---

5 This often takes the form of an association of "library friends".
6 There is a current movement in the United States and Canada to eliminate fines in libraries.

Some libraries do not require a full refund, but rather a flat fee. In addition to libraries that charge a registration fee for borrowing, others issue a free user's card, as is the case in many public libraries in Switzerland. However, there is a downside to this apparently free service (which exists for the use of the premises and the collections on site or at home); the lending of DVD or Blu-ray films and access to the Internet are generally charged for, sometimes symbolically, to regulate the flow of users. Another downside is the services made available (access to professional information and advice, work and consultation areas, access to specialized information using databases and electronic periodicals, reading the press, listening to music, access to exhibitions and so on), which appear to be services that are taken for granted, but which are not always so, because they need to be financed in some way. Let us take the example of scientific documentation and periodicals in university libraries, which represent significant portions of the budget: most users (students, as well as lecturers or researchers) find it normal to access this specialized information from the campus or at home using VPN access, and do not seek to know who manages these resources, who allocates an essential part of its budget to these purchases or who manages remote access, in other words, the libraries.

2.3.2. *Why pay for information?*

In principle, free information and access for all is highly desirable and is recommended by the Declaration of Principles and Action Lines of the World Summit on the Information Society (WSIS[7]). In reality, there are several arguments in favor of fee-based information. The first is, as we have seen, that there is no such thing as free information – this is an illusion: at the origin of all information, there is an author, then a distribution channel and then receivers. The production–distribution of information is therefore based on an intellectual production at the origin, and then on an infrastructure, often transparent to the users, but which is not free. The Google search engine stores billions of pieces of information on its servers, accessible through a simplistic interface represented by a field to be

---

7 https://www.itu.int/net/wsis/docs/geneva/official/dop-fr.html.

filled in. Google is attractive, as are other search engines, because they cost nothing to the community, unlike libraries. They are constantly evolving, which is another attractive trait, and the user ends up being dependent on search engines, which provide a free service apparently without obligation, apart from the fact that the engine in question retrieves the query data. The ease of querying is so great that it is perceived as being obvious by most people and finally... free. Nothing could be further from the truth, as Google is paid by the advertising that appears when the results of a query are listed: algorithms and artificial intelligence then play their full role in proposing results to the user according to their tastes and recorded preferences. The social network Facebook does the same thing by cross-referencing the different personal data stored in a profile. The pinnacle is reached since these companies are listed on the stock exchange with capitalizations of several billion dollars... So somewhere, there is always someone who pays, at one end or another of the information chain[8].

From the point of view of the information services, the question of paid information and services no longer arises. It has been accepted as a fact for several decades. It is also seen by documentalists as a means of recognizing their work in the organizations in which they are employed.

Working on current events, practicing monitoring and using sophisticated tools such as professional databases, they help companies make decisions. Free information is used, but is less valued than paid information because:

– the fee is seen as a guarantee of commitment, for example, for the validation of the information provided or the formalization of the processes of implementation of a service;

– paying is a guarantee of "after-sales service", the information provider – in this case, the documentalist – is responsible for what he/she delivers;

---

[8] Google and Facebook, however, are beginning to be subject to taxes in some states, following numerous lawsuits and hearings.

– the fee can be considered to be an "orthodox" mode of funding compared to other "unorthodox" modes of funding, such as advertising or market capitalization;

– the fee as the price to be paid for information or a service delivered from "entertainment" and not making the consumer and his/her habits the product.

Information that was previously difficult to obtain because it was not disseminated, such as gray literature (reports, activity reports, dissertations, theses, patents), is now more easily accessible on the information networks because it is digitized. However, there are still a few niches where information is not free of charge: this is the case for financial information or information concerning standards and patents.

2.4. The Internet and digital technology

With the development of the Internet, social networks and search engines, information has taken on a new dimension: it is produced, disseminated and reproduced *ad infinitum* and for free. The old economic models have been overturned in scientific publishing, the press and books, so new models must therefore be invented. The culture of free access is now embedded in people's minds, but one question remains: how to remunerate creators and authors?

The Internet has, to an extent, taken the place of libraries, which also offer information almost free of charge, but with much less impact than the Internet (we are not referring to the services offered by libraries here). It has penetrated everyone's way of life; it has become an indispensable, unavoidable part of professional and private life: schools, universities and businesses, for example, are now accompanied by terms such as e-learning, e-governance and e-administration. The Internet and digital technology are therefore raising the question of the role of libraries today. Where do libraries fit within this digital environment? This book demonstrates that their role is essential.

Many other questions remain unanswered. However, it is quite clear, at the end of this recomposition of the panorama between free and paid information, that the actors are no longer the same, that they intervene differently in the digital information production chain. There is no doubt that this situation will evolve before a real balance can be found and the sentence "not everything can be free" can be countered.

2.5. Towards new economic models

While the last century seemed to establish a clear boundary between paid and free information, new economic models are now emerging that are less clear-cut, particularly with the notion of "knowledge commons". Some examples include:

– streaming music or books;

– the *freemium*[9] model for libraries;

– video on demand (VOD);

– replay or catch-up TV, allowing the viewing of television programs on a deferred basis;

– Open Data, some of which, such as Open Educational Resources (OER)[10], have alternative funding;

– Wikipedia and the collaborative model.

2.6. The theory of knowledge commons[11]

For most economists, information and its dissemination used to be linked to the material dimension of the media, implying the notion of

---

9 "Freemium" is a contraction of "free" and "premium": in addition to the free services offered to the user, services with high added value are also offered. The term was popularized by the business journalist Anderson. Anderson, C. (2009). *Free: The Future of a Radical Price.* Hyperion, New York.

10 http://www.unesco.org/new/fr/communication-and-information/access-to-knowledge/open-educational-resources/.

11 http://www.savoirscom1.info and Communs/Commons; http://paigrain.debatpublic.net.

scarcity and cost: using copyright to protect publishers appeared to be obvious, in order to deal with the fixed costs of producing copies or the technical distribution system. With copyright remunerating their creation, the book distribution chain would be organized. According to economists, the shrinking of traditional information media is leading to the possibility of remunerating other forms of creative.

The theory of knowledge commons studies the way in which communities that collectively manage shareable resources find forms of governance that allow these resources to be maintained. This is not without danger or threat: a resource can be privatized and be no longer freely accessible and so is then for the sole benefit of the owner. The privatization of knowledge is a recent trend. The resource may not be easily accessible if the Internet is congested, under attack or subject to access restrictions. A "commons" can be constituted, for example, by Internet protocols (IP) and usage rules. Threats to knowledge commons include spam, erroneous Wikipedia articles, scientific fraud and conflicts in knowledge-creating communities. The theory of commons promotes collective wealth through the dissemination of knowledge that can be shared. David Bollier, an American economist and pioneer of the commons cause, defines the commons paradigm as follows:

> An evolving set of operational models of self-governance [...] needs satisfaction and responsible management that combine the economic and the social, the collective and the personal. Those who apply this theory – called "*commoners*" – whether in ecology or digital technology, are in deliberative and participatory practice[12].

The development of digital technology, with all that it implies in terms of the ease of exchange and sharing, truly raises the question of information governance.

---

12 Bollier, D. (2014). *Think Like a Commoner: A Short Introduction to the Life of the Commons*. New Society Publishers, Gabriola Island.

3

The Evolution of the Library Space

3.1. From the perspective of creation and innovation

It is interesting to note the contradiction that libraries are becoming increasingly virtual, but are also well frequented by the public. However, rather than talking about a contradiction, let us talk about complementarity between the physical and virtual worlds. The debate that took place in France on extending opening hours illustrates the importance of the physical place. This is due, in this case, to several factors:

– the need for a neutral place at the intersection between social and cultural activity centers, the house of culture, youth centers and seniors' clubs, among others. The library is the perfect place to create social links where people of different origins, cultures and ages can meet;

– the stated need for places where students can study, especially in large urban centers: for economic reasons, in view of the high cost of rent, students often do not have fixed workplaces or have accommodation unsuitable for study (shared accommodation, cramped premises, the need to work in groups). The use of places such as the *Bibliothèque Publique d'Information* (Bpi), the Paris public information library, among others, demonstrates this real need;

– the need for a place that combines access to different resources, or spaces that can be adapted to accommodate working groups and put students in contact with companies, for instance: the success of learning centers – Lilliad at the University of Lille[1] and the Rolex Learning Center at the Swiss Federal Institute of Technology (*École Polytechnique Fédérale de Lausanne,* EPFL[2]) – is a good example.

Today, we are in a situation where virtual and face-to-face models are increasingly coexisting. The library, a physical place, is not about to be dethroned, especially by digital technology, because it offers many possibilities: few places in a city or on a university campus offer so many facilities (social, human, in terms of paper or digital resources, coworking). Projects for new buildings, or the redevelopment of other places, currently abound all over the planet and there are regular announcements of spectacular new libraries, in China, Qatar and Europe, for example.

At the same time, digital libraries have a great future ahead of them[3].

3.2. From the third place to DIY

Among the spaces of creation and innovation, let us discuss the library as a "third place"[4]. The concept of the third place is a generic one, grouping together leisure or learning spaces at the midpoint between the home (the first place) and the working world (the second place): these are coworking (shared working) spaces, "Fab Labs" and "hackerspaces", which will be developed below.

The general public, as well as companies, are able to innovate, design and implement projects and learn about and train for the digital world. Information services and libraries are increasingly seen, and rightly so, as places of interaction and experimentation. They are conceived as spaces for the production of knowledge based on participation. One possible way forward is for them to become places where citizens experiment and interact. Citizens, documentalists and

---

[1] https://lilliad.univ-lille.fr/.
[2] https://www.epfl.ch/campus/visitors/fr/batiments-phares/rolex-learning-center/.
[3] See Part 3.
[4] See also the preface by Michel Gorin who talks about this notion.

librarians then become creators: of films, documentaries, pieces of music, video games and so on.

Do-it-yourself (DIY) is the philosophy. Learning takes place through on-site (or off-site) workshops that often lead to digital creation. These are what we now call Fab Labs or hackerspaces.

In overview, a Fab Lab or "Fabrication Laboratory" is a collaborative factory. It is open to all and allows the public to produce, create and design prototypes of innovative objects, alone or in groups, using a range of available tools, such as 3D printers, soldering irons and electronic components. Fab Labs follow a precise charter and form international networks where everyone shares, exchanges and collaborates on their know-how.

In France, there are many examples of Fab Labs: a map shows their location and an association has been created[5]. France is the leading country for Fab Labs worldwide, with more than 400 listed, according to the *Mission Société Numérique*[6]. There are different types of Fab Labs:

– Media Lab, or media laboratory: differs from the Fab Lab, in that, instead of making all kinds of objects, the Media Lab public exclusively produces digital and multimedia content. Workshops and conferences on digital and multimedia, such as "social networks" workshops or open radio platforms, are also offered. The Media Lab is therefore focused on the issue of media (information, videos, images);

– Info Lab, or information laboratory: a space where the public is informed about the control and use of digital data. Through workshops and conference debates, multiple themes, raising ethical, legal and economic questions, are addressed (Open Data, Big Data, personal data);

– Living Lab: offers the general public the opportunity to test new products before they go to market. Here, participants are evaluating,

---

5 Scientific Council of the French *Fab Lab* Network (2019). *Livre blanc. Panorama des Fab Labs en France* [Online]. Available at: http://wiki.fablab.fr/index.php/Livre_Blanc.
6 https://labo.societenumerique.gouv.fr/2018/05/07/pres-de-400-fablabs-france/.

rather than producing, giving their opinion and exchanging views on the objects of tomorrow;

– Maker Space: more informal and autonomous than most Fab Labs, this is a space where people who already have a common interest in digital technology and DIY get together to create innovative tools. To do this, the maker space provides them with a set of digital tools (such as 3D printers and machine tools).

3.2.1. *Digital public spaces (Espaces Publics Numériques, EPN) in France*

In France, EPNs are set up for the digital development of territories (departments, regions) and are open to all. They provide an introduction to digital tools, services and innovations through a variety of activities, such as meetings, debates, group initiation or production workshops, individual mediation and free consultation. The mediation aspect is developed with qualified support to encourage the appropriation of technologies and uses of fixed and mobile Internet. They are designed to be true resource centers. EPNs can therefore develop activities related to digital proximity production technologies. They can also organize actions aimed at developing control of information from administrations and companies, enabling citizens to appropriate this data and create the new services they will need on a daily basis (within the framework of Info Labs):

– The Hackerspace is, like the maker space, organized in an informal and autonomous way; but it finds singularity in its activity, which is essentially centered around the world of data processing. As true hackers, participants meet to create, modify or evaluate computer programs, using free software and alternative media in particular.

– The Repair Cafe invites the general public to repair clothes, furniture and other used objects in a collaborative and friendly space. Thanks to the support of volunteers who are experts in DIY, Repair Cafes are becoming places of mutual collaboration, where everyone, in their own way, battles against the programmed obsolescence of everyday objects.

– Coworking Spaces are one of the best known third places. Generally rented by the day, these workspaces allow self-employed people (solopreneurs and freelancers) to work away from home with the possibility of forming synergies with other coworkers. Mainly configured in open space, coworking allows everyone access to the usual facilities of a company, in a friendly environment without direct hierarchical pressure.

Below are some examples of EPN achievements, which are similar to, or which constitute digital or online mediation actions:

– introductions to the Internet and multimedia;

– improvements and accompaniments to digital projects;

– coworking, remote working and training, MOOCs and so on;

– Internet job searches, socioprofessional networks and so on;

– administrative procedures and e-administration;

– mobile tools and uses (smartphones, tablets, e-readers, applications);

– Fab Labs, Info Labs, Living Labs, Recycl'Art, Upcycling and so on;

– robotics and computer programming workshops;

– Wi-Fi access and stand-alone access;

– digital resources (such as participants, materials, documentation, engineering, expertise and advice);

– connected objects (such as discovery, handling and creation).

There are public digital spaces right across France, thanks to local authorities. They help us to reduce the geographical, cultural, social and economic inequalities that can exist within a given territory and are an effective way of fighting the digital divide, both material and cultural. Five thousand public digital spaces are open in France, with facilitators[7].

Box 1.1. *Digital public spaces*

---

7 http://www.netpublic.fr/net-public/espaces-publics-numeriques/presentation/.

3.2.2. *Some examples of Fab Labs in American libraries*

Neil Gershenfeld[8] is the originator of the Fab Lab concept and now runs The Fab Academy[9]. He is a professor at MIT (Massachusetts Institute of Technology).

Some examples of American Fab Labs:

– the Cleveland Public Library has set up "Tech Central"[10] which includes a computer lab, a 3D printer and a TechToyBox, with all the latest tech gadgets, access to a personalized cloud – MyCloud, and so on;

– other libraries have special areas for teenagers, such as Anythink Brighton[11];

– Sacramento Library offers a workshop for writing and self-publishing – *i-street*[12].

Box 1.2. *Examples of Fab Labs in the United States*

Previously, only the physical spaces of creation were detailed and reviewed. However, the creation and innovation spaces are also digital, which is developed later, in Part 3, "Library Tools and Technology".

3.3. Learning spaces or learning centers

While the spaces for creation and innovation discussed in Chapter 2 most often concern so-called public reading spaces (with the third place), university libraries are also evolving towards learning spaces or *learning centers*. Far from being a fashionable phenomenon, they correspond to a change in the needs and behaviors of students and teachers, as well as to the implementation of innovative teaching

---

8 https://en.wikipedia.org/wiki/Neil_Gershenfeld.
9 http://fabacademy.org/.
10 https://cpl.org/aboutthelibrary/subjectscollections/techcentral/.
11 https://www.anythinklibraries.org/location/anythink-brighton.
12 https://www.saclibrary.org/Education/Tech-Creation/I-Street-Press.

methods linked to society and business. They offer an attractive and seductive image, both in the eyes of those who frequent them and in the eyes of decision-makers, financiers and politicians. These places sometimes become the emblem or the brand image of the establishment that hosts them.

These places are characterized by:

– a strong identity, based on a service brand: the Rolex Learning Center in Lausanne, Lilliad at the University of Lille, or the Hexagone at the University of Aix-Marseille come to mind;

– the bringing together in one place of a wide range of information contents and services;

– the emphasis placed on comfort (furniture, circulation areas, light, colors) and reception (reception desks; trained reception staff);

– services offered include technical assistance, loan of equipment, private or collective spaces and places to relax and eat.

The mediation of information professionals is an essential complement.

One of the notable advantages of learning centers is that they better integrate the library with teaching, since sharing of teaching spaces and multiple exchanges with spaces dedicated to entrepreneurs is possible, for example. Printed material does not disappear, however, but is made accessible in spaces dedicated to collections, freely accessible to students and teachers. Cooperation between librarians and teachers is strengthened.

3.4. The Smart Libraries concept

Joachim Schöpfel, researcher in information and communication sciences, defines the concept of Smart Libraries in relation to that of Smart Cities[13]. The smart city is hyperconnected and designed in a sustainable environment, at the service of its citizens. It uses data,

---

13 Schöpfel, J. (2018). Smart Libraries. *Infrastructures*, 3, 43.

especially Big Data, for this purpose[14]. How does the library fit in with this? The concept of a learning center previously outlined (as well as the green library, designed in an environmental and sustainable way) is quite close to it. Information technologies are indeed dominant, with a preoccupation with the central place of the user. J. Schöpfel details the concept with four dimensions:

– intelligent services;

– intelligent individuals;

– the smart place;

– intelligent governance.

The more a library develops new services, thereby increasing access to information, the more it contributes to the production of knowledge and the return on public investment increases. Another consideration is that the social value of the library is enhanced.

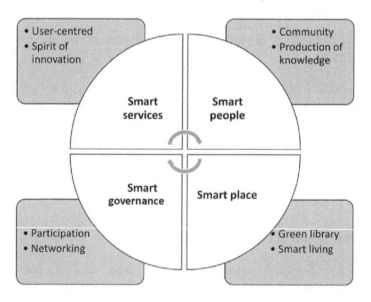

Figure 3.1. *The fourth dimension of Smart Libraries by Joachim Schöpfel*

---

14 More than a hundred cities around the world have declared themselves "smart cities", with Singapore leading the way.

The concept of Smart Libraries does not necessarily apply to all libraries and will not solve all problems: it must truly be part of a global context, that of a connected city. J. Schöpfel concludes by saying that libraries should be renamed in the light of their own evolution.

3.5. Wellness spaces

Libraries and information services promote the personal and professional development of individuals through the opportunities offered for lifelong information, reading, training and education, even – especially? – within the context of a company or institution.

These services therefore contribute to the general wellness of an organization, a living space or, more broadly, a city. We will see later that the concept of mediation perfectly applies to the definition of wellness and is even essential for its full application[15].

Bill Hettler[16] defined the six dimensions of wellness, shown in Figure 3.2: physical, intellectual, emotional, spiritual, social and occupational.

In order for services to qualify as wellness spaces, and to meet the six criteria set out, they must emphasize, develop or intensify their reception policy, with friendly and welcoming staff: libraries often impress regulars as well as non-regulars or non-users, even if it is only by taking the step of approaching them or asking a question. If people know or perceive that they are going to feel welcomed, access is made easier. In the same way, the collection space should make people want to come in and spend time there: the emphasis is therefore on the circulation areas, the furniture, the layout, the colors, the light, the ventilation of the premises and so on. A number of professions can be mobilized around these concepts, such as interior architects, graphic designers and signage specialists.

---

15 See Part 4.
16 http://www.hettler.com/.

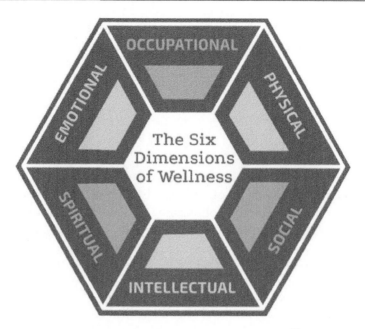

Figure 3.2. *The six dimensions of wellness*[17]

There are many initiatives to develop the notion of wellness in libraries. Quite apart from the attitudes and behaviors of the professionals who work there and welcome the public, it is a question of offering fun activities:

– for young audiences, story times and other readings have been held for many years. Playful workshops can also be offered;

– games for young adults (escape games are very popular);

– activities proposed by the cultural mediators (such as conferences and visits by writers) are also not new.

In university libraries, students could be included in reflections on wellness, with a view to setting up anti-stress workshops with relaxing activities; snacks can be offered to students and games proposed. New

---

17 Hettler, M.D. (1976). Six dimensions of wellness model. *National Wellness Institute, Inc.* Available at: https://www.nationalwellness.org/page/Six_Dimensions.

experiments are being tried, such as organizing rest areas (for naps) in libraries, particularly for students, such as at the health library at Jean-Monnet University, in Saint-Étienne[18]. The university library in Angers has set up a "home-like" concept by furnishing the old DVD area with furniture from Emmaüs or Ikea, which resembles what students already know and is reminiscent of home life. Blankets are also loaned out[19].

Librarians offer multiple activities, sometimes without any real link to the original function of the library, which is then considered as a place in itself, open, adapting or inserting itself into the world around it.

Wellness is not a concept that can develop itself; a number of conditions must be met in order to achieve it. The place and its layout play a major role in this, as does the general attitude of the professionals.

3.6. Reception areas: a user-oriented approach

Users are placed at the center of the library facility. They do not always have the means to access the collections or the information they need. By adopting a user-oriented approach, the library engages all the means at its disposal to best meet the information needs expressed.

Every institution must cultivate its image in the eyes of the public: the reception service, which performs several functions (reception, information, guidance, information retrieval, user training and so on), is the first point of contact with the user and represents the institution. Delivery of the service offered is based on a quality approach:

– quality of reception (friendliness, sense of welcome, listening and so on);

---

18 https://www.lemonde.fr/campus/article/2017/02/07/une-salle-pour-rejoindre-les-bras-de-morphee-a-l-universite_5076002_4401467.html.
19 http://blog.univ-angers.fr/buapro/2018/04/04/prototype-damenagement-comme-a-la-maison-a-la-bu-dangers/.

– quality of information provided (relevance, timeliness, completeness and so on);

– visibility of the service (signage, logo, colors adopted and so on).

The more considered the reception service concept, the better the image of the institution in the eyes of the user. User orientation is a holistic approach within the institution and is much more than a goal, a culture, a promise or an advertising slogan. User orientation is a strategy that affects the whole institution and its services, with a particular mode of organization, as well as an adapted mode of management. It is fundamentally the opposite of product orientation, which proposes the same product for a set of potential users; in fact, user orientation aims to individualize and personalize the service or provision proposed, to adapt it as closely as possible to the user's expectations. In this sense, a reception service must meet specific needs.

For documentation services in semi-public or private sector institutions, the situation is quite different, as they have to continually justify their expenditure and compete with new technologies. Information is truly an economic good with a certain value. The current information context is changing and evolving daily: how can information professionals react and find appropriate solutions? In this sense, user orientation brings constructive elements:

– it allows for targeting of users and their needs;

– it helps to continuously improve the added value of products and services;

– it enables partnerships to develop;

– it is an aid to reflection with a view to expanding and renewing the range of services and products.

In the end, user orientation is a concrete aid to innovation.

The reception service is a trump card to be played in a user-oriented approach: it brings real added value to the overall information offering. Archive services, libraries, media libraries, computer libraries and company information services all have one thing in common: they require a reception, information and inquiry point for both internal and external users. Depending on their orientation (public or private, cultural, semi-public or semi-private, profit or non-profit, associative, open to the outside world or only responding to internal requests), the reception service responds to different demands and offers diversified information tools. However, the overall philosophy of this service remains the same, namely to inform, advise and guide the user as best as possible.

3.7. The use of the library space

From another point of view, the question of the place and the space offered leads to the question: should a library only be a place of study, of living, of simple passage or all three at once?

These spaces are generally designed in such a way that the public feels at ease, can move around easily and freely and can access the collections and tools offered. It is certain that today's libraries – and therefore librarians – are not content with meeting the public on the Web, but are developing all possible strategies to meet the public wherever they are:

– Schiphol Airport (Amsterdam) has opened a permanent high-tech library[20];

– the city of London is developing living spaces that bring together a range of services around the library, such as crèches;

– the National Library of Singapore hosts many business seminars for business people[21] and a green library for children (the Tree Library)[22].

There are many other examples. In Switzerland, the Rolex Learning Center in Lausanne[23] and the Schmidheiny Science Library

---

20 http://www.rnw.nl/english/article/worlds-first-airport-library-schiphol-amsterdam.
21 http://www.nlb.gov.sg/.
22 http://www.nlb.gov.sg/labs/my-tree-house-green-library-for-kids-information/.
23 http://www.rolexlearningcenter.ch/.

at the University of Geneva[24] offer redesigned spaces for reading, consultation and relaxation: comfortable furniture (the Rolex even offers transportable footstools for its users so that they can settle wherever they wish); Wi-Fi access; large circulation spaces and openness to the outside through large bay windows; coffee and catering at the entrance; free access to the archived collections thanks to Compactus systems; group work spaces; presentation rooms: everything is done so that the user feels comfortable and above all permanently "occupies" the space[25].

Opening hours for library sites are of crucial importance: the current trend in Europe, especially in university libraries[26], is towards extended opening hours, generally from 8 am until 10 pm or even midnight, in the evening, at weekends and on certain holidays. To address the question of the cost, which would be very high if librarians were to work these hours, this is solved by hiring students or monitors and by offering less elaborate services. On the other hand, some public libraries have had their opening hours reduced for budgetary reasons, which is always harmful. North American libraries have been successfully testing 24-hour opening, day and night, with no staff assigned at night: this system is obviously based on trust and is possible in very specific settings, such as research libraries or hospitals. The question of opening hours is also crucial in the event of an economic or housing crisis: in this case, libraries play a significant social role.

---

24 http://www.unige.ch/biblio/sciences/infos/sciences2.html.

25 The Rolex Learning Center is so busy that some of the work rooms in the old library have had to be reopened.

26 The French Ministry for Higher Education, Valérie Pécresse, presented her plan for the renewal of university libraries in February 2010. This plan includes, in the short term, the massive expansion of opening hours. In total, 31 libraries with the *NoctamBU* accreditation will be open for more than 65 hours per week in 2010. See: http://www.enseignementsup-recherche.gouv.fr/cid50597/des-bibliotheques-universitaires-ouvertes-plus-longtemps.html. The Orsenna Report of February 2018, "Voyage au pays des bibliothèques : lire aujourd'hui, lire demain", reinforces this idea of extended opening hours. See: https://www.culture.gouv.fr/Espace-documentation/Rapports/Voyage-au-pays-des-bibliotheques.-Lire-aujourd'hui-lire-demain.

As a social place, libraries are used as places of experimentation in some cases (even if the term "experimentation" is a bit strong), such as during the "migrant crisis": German librarians reacted very quickly by offering help and support.

It is therefore interesting to note – through these different examples – that the physical user is as important as the virtual user; it is no longer possible to separate them. They are often one and the same and are used to receiving the same type of services. This is the visible and tangible result of current marketing approaches that are bringing libraries into an era closer to the market economy – and no longer just a cultural economy – in order to retain their audiences and attract new ones. Far from lagging behind, libraries and information services are highly inventive and innovative in this area.

3.8. Green libraries

Ecology is fashionable (and is perhaps a fundamental phenomenon), if we believe the results of the last European elections or the words of young people who are taking to the streets to finally awaken climate awareness. What are libraries doing on this topic? Do they, or rather the decision makers, financiers and politicians, feel concerned? Lobbying would be very useful here.

The "Green Library" movement is not new. It originated in the United States, but is not only active there: a few years ago, the National Library of Singapore created the My Tree House Library at the Central Library[27], with a view to raising awareness of this theme among children. The International Federation of Library Associations and Institutions (IFLA) has also been active in this area, regularly addressing sustainability issues at its conferences and publishing a book entitled *Libraries Going Green*[28]. It awards an annual prize, the

---

27 https://www.littledayout.com/2013/06/01/my-tree-house-worlds-first-green-library-for-kids/.
28 https://www.ifla.org/publications/ifla-publications-series-177.

IFLA Green Library Award[29], and this is one of the main points of the UN 2030 Agenda[30].

What forms can this take in the library? First of all, in the design of spaces (circulation, ventilation, brightness of the premises), in the materials used, then in more responsible and less energy-consuming computing, as well as in the awareness of employees and the public. The management of collections can be an important element in this policy (which comes down to the question of digital vs. paper).

---

29 https://www.ifla.org/node/10159.
30 https://www.un.org/sustainabledevelopment/development-agenda/.

4

Legal Changes

4.1. GDPR: European data protection regulations, as applied to libraries

One of the societal changes currently in progress is the strengthening of the legal protection of individuals, particularly personal data. With the development of social networks, this data is subject to important economic stakes that the European Union wishes to better control and frame. To this end, the European General Data Protection Regulation (GDPR) was introduced in May 2018 as a continuation of the French Data Protection Act of 1978 and strengthens citizens' control over the use that can be made of their data. They must, for example, give their consent to receive advertisements or newsletters. Private companies and public institutions are implementing GDPR.

A library processes or collects data on its users in the course of its business and therefore has specific obligations to guarantee the protection of the data entrusted to it. In the case where the library is under the supervision of a local authority, as part of a public service delegation:

> It is the administrative authority (for example, the mayor for the commune or the president of the departmental council for the department), which takes the decision to accept the residual risks and how they have been managed. It must be committed to a continuous

improvement of security. When the teleservice uses certain technical devices (authentication, encryption, electronic signature, and so on), the administrative authority must comply with the rules defined in the annexes to the general security relations (*Règlement Général de Sécurité*, RGS)[1].

This regulation aims to give back control to individuals over the use of their personal data collected by the online services they use.

4.1.1. *The fields of application*

GDPR applies in relation to the personal data of each individual: any individual wishing to register for the library provides their personal data and the loans or consultations that they will subsequently make are also part of this. The individual is identified by their membership card number, which allows their data to be retrieved within the library management system (LMS). How is that data collected?

There are several possibilities:

– from the registration using a paper form: last name, first name, address, phone number, sex, age, email;

– from the member record entered into the LMS: last name, first name, address, telephone number, sex, age, email, documents borrowed, reservations;

– using a Wi-Fi connection: sender, recipient, time, duration, place of origin of communications, technical connection data (MAC address, IP (Internet Protocol) address, manufacturer's number);

– using a tablet: last name, first name, card number from a register;

– using a computer: member card number;

– by connecting to the library's website: reader account, IP address, email.

---

1 CNIL (2018). La Sécurité des données des administrés, November 30 [Online]. Available at: https://www.cnil.fr/en/node/22892.

The *Commission nationale de l'informatique et des libertés* (CNIL) has defined a simplified standard (NS-009) which includes:

– last name, first names, address, year of birth, professional category, telephone number;

– the characteristics of the loan or communication: designation of the work (title, name of the author, publisher and so on) or of the archival document (catalogue or classification number, date, renewal date).

This data is processed by the library for different purposes such as lending of documents, financial management and the production of general statistics, which are not personalized. However, there are other actors who process this data.

4.1.2. *Data processing and hosting*

Without actually realizing it, the library is not the only entity collecting user data. Other entities include:

– the local authority through the Information Services Department (ISD);

– the authority's Internet service provider;

– the portal provider who hosts the site;

– the ILMS (Integrated Library Management System) provider, if it owns the servers;

– providers of digital resources accessible from the portal. The list of subcontractors must be produced and they must comply with GDPR rules. Their responsibility may be engaged in case of failure.

This raises the question of data hosting. Several solutions for hosting data are possible:

– the IT infrastructure of the city, the university or the company;

– the servers of the provider hosting the library's website;

– the servers of digital resource providers.

Regarding the location of the hosting, so far as libraries are concerned, there is little risk that this will be outside the European Union. The duration of data storage is standardized: technical connection data is kept for a maximum of 12 months, according to national legislation.

Regarding connection data, European law provides for a retention period of no more than 14 days:

– the borrower's data is kept for the duration of the service (the time of the loan) and is deleted one year after the end of the latest loan;

– the information relating to each loan is deleted at the end of the fourth month following the return of the document.

4.2. Protection of personal data

Article 35 of GDPR states that the protection of personal data requires appropriate organizational measures to be taken, in order to guarantee a level of security appropriate to the risks[2].

In order to ensure data security, it is necessary to:

– provide for encryption of Wi-Fi networks;

– secure access to the BIOS[3] of the computers made available;

– prevent the booting of a third-party operating system using a USB stick;

– secure access to connection logs;

– provide a strong enough password for the BIOS to prevent changes to the system configuration;

– limit the storage time of documents awaiting printing to a few minutes, in order to avoid the disclosure of sensitive data to third parties;

---

2 https://www.cnil.fr/fr/reglement-europeen-protection-donnees/chapitre4#Article32.
3 Basic input output system.

– implement the TLS[4] protocol on the site, in order to encrypt data and requests.

While the current environment is crucial to the evolution of libraries and information services, bringing them squarely into the real economy, at the heart of the concerns of politicians and decision-makers, management and new theories are also currently driving a significant change in this sector. This is the subject of Part 2.

---

4 The purpose of the TLS protocol is to secure communications between two applications – usually a web server and a browser. This protocol is widely used and compatible with most web browsers.

PART 2

Human Resources and Management

5

New Management Theories Applicable to Libraries

It is no longer possible to manage a team or teams of employees today in the same way as 20 years ago. They have become more demanding with regard to their work and their hierarchy, wishing to be involved in the overall management of a service, to be stakeholders in the decision-making process or, in any event, to be informed. Vertical management no longer happens, except in some companies or in very hierarchical companies.

Among current management theories, some are obviously more attractive than others, as well as more applicable to everyday life. We will thus see:

– participatory management;

– management by benevolence or well-treatment;

– management by empathy;

– change management;

– project management.

New methods, such as Design Thinking, User Experience or agile methods, are also detailed.

5.1. Participatory management

Participatory management has been on the rise for several years, and it marks a real step forward in human resource management. It is derived from, or is similar to, project management, which is also a participatory management method.

5.1.1. *The five principles of participatory management*

1) Involving staff: without continually imposing it, participatory management encourages the involvement of the staff in the decision-making process. The team leader encourages staff to set goals and make decisions to achieve them. This may involve ideas such as a new distribution of the library's collections within the spaces, the introduction of an additional service to the public or the networking of resources.

2) Implementing a personal development policy: participatory management relies on the development of communication within the organization and on the establishment of favorable working conditions. Stimulating staff to listen, share and collaborate helps to first develop individual confidence, then collective confidence, which ultimately strengthens team spirit and improves overall functioning. In addition, many skills and abilities can be developed in the library, particularly social, as well as technical skills.

3) Knowing how to delegate: part of the power of the management team (managers and supervisors) is delegated to employees and collaborators. This delegation, which is necessary for participatory management to function, is progressive and is based on two principles:

– subsidiarity, whereby each team member is empowered to make a decision at their own level, without the intervention of a superior. All these decisions will be communicated to management, which will integrate them into its own strategy. What is allowed to be decided at a lower level should not be decided by the higher level;

– compliance with strategy, to which all decisions taken are subject.

4) Entrusting problem solving to the teams involved: participatory management empowers teams to solve problems at their level. Management is only consulted if a suitable solution is not found.

5) Establishing regulation: individual and collective regulation mechanisms must be put in place. While the right to make mistakes is recognized, self-control and regulation mechanisms contribute to the effectiveness of participatory management by coordinating teams, while making them autonomous and accountable. Jacques Leplat indicates:

> When we say that a process is regulated, we imply, at least, that it is controlled and organized, even if we do not specify how. In this fuzzy meaning, a regulated process is opposed to a more or less erratic process[1].

5.1.2. *The qualities required for participatory management*

1) Listening: the manager listens to the needs and expectations of colleagues. This real listening enables links within the team to be improved and strengthened and possible tensions to be eliminated.

2) Communication: effective communication must be established between management and employees in order to avoid misconceptions, misunderstandings and to reduce conflicts as much as possible. The dissemination of information is an important element in effective communication.

3) Respect for others: even more so than communication, respect for others is a value that should not be forgotten. By valuing the work of each person, whatever their position in the hierarchy, the team can move forward and learn from each other.

---

1 Leplat, J. (2006). La Notion de régulation dans l'analyse de l'activité. *Pistes*, 8(1), 1 [Online]. Available at: https://journals.openedition.org/pistes/3101.

4) Dialogue: the purpose of dialogue is to create the conditions for listening to opinions and suggestions that will facilitate the achievement of objectives.

5) Delegation: delegation aims to give each person a level of responsibility in which they can make decisions without the intervention of their hierarchy.

Participatory management attaches particular importance to the participation of employees in the life of the institution. Far from being a theory, it is the lever for implementing change. The model of participatory management continually evolves and can be adapted to any type of organization. Many small companies adopt it, and it is a total success, given the direct involvement of all.

As an extension of, or as a complement to, participatory management, management by benevolence finds its rightful place.

5.2. Management by benevolence or well-treatment

According to the Larousse dictionary:

> Benevolence is a disposition of mind inclining to understanding, to indulgence of others[2].

Benevolence is not a naive humanistic concept; it is the product of a certain way of life and management that is increasingly at the heart of employees' concerns. Benevolence is a component of ethical behavior.

In companies, the benevolent management style contrasts with the pyramidal or vertical management style, which is more intrusive from a work perspective and more "controlling", indicating less trust in the employees. Beyond the individual, the whole company must be benevolent by way of, for example, an adapted human resources policy. Why is this so? According to a number of studies, this is

---

2 *Larousse Dictionary*, 2018.

because, in the years to come, the attachment of individuals to their company (Generations Y and Z) will be increasingly weak.

People will choose their company, rather than the other way around. This fact, combined with the mass retirement of the baby boomers, means that French companies must prepare for what German companies are experiencing: seduce in order to recruit. To prepare for the future, and to have the best employees, public and private institutions must prepare themselves and, for some, change.

Six keywords are used to define benevolence: association, listening, management, development, smiling and responsibility:

– Association: in large teams, it is difficult to involve all employees in collective decision-making, but it is a good idea to share, discuss and reach a form of consensus. It is, in any case, important to inform. In small- and medium-sized teams, communication can be more direct.

– Listening: it is essential to listen to the manager, because it is their teams who face the problems and it is they who most often have solutions to propose. For an employee, it is also more motivating to give an opinion and to feel that it counts. For the manager, this attentive listening allows them to clarify their choices and is essential in order to establish a lasting relationship of trust.

– Management: managing with benevolence means behaving on an equal level with our employees and not privileging one group over another, or one person over another. Otherwise, the risk is that managers will surround themselves with a small group of people and fail to see the problems of the whole team.

– Development: mistakes are sometimes made. Today, we no longer punish as we used to. Making mistakes is part of the order of things and of teamwork in general: everyone, including management, must acknowledge their mistakes and ensure that they are transformed positively.

– Smiling: having a positive, engaging attitude helps us to establish a climate of trust and open discussion within a team.

– Responsibility: sometimes there is bad news for the manager to announce: maybe a reduction in the budget or perhaps a freeze on recruitment. Even if there is bad news to be announced, a manager who communicates is always appreciated by the team if it's done with knowledge, tact and respect.

Benevolence generates positive energy. Developing this attitude in any type of institution or service helps us to reduce difficulties and tensions between people who are treated in an equivalent manner. It may seem obvious to say that the human being is essential, but it is necessary to reaffirm this.

5.3. Empathy, a management method?

Let us specify at the outset that the notion of empathy is not synonymous with that of benevolence, discussed above. The term was first used in 1873 by the German philosopher Robert Vischer and literally means "feeling into".

It would then be developed in the sense of understanding what others feel and a term more recently defined in France:

> Benevolence: the intuitive ability to put oneself in the place of another, to perceive how they feel[3].

This relatively new concept opens up the field of emotions and the senses. It also means the sharing and contagion of emotions between individuals. We will speak of an empathic link.

In terms of management, traditional methods do not allow for empathy. However, many companies or institutions are now using project management or agile methods that require a human approach, very different from the hierarchical mode; otherwise, in most cases, a project to be developed, requiring a high level of participation from the teams, will be doomed to failure. Empathy plays an essential role here.

---

3 *Le Petit Larousse*, 2018.

To be open to others – in terms of team management and therefore from the point of view of the leader – it is necessary for them to be open to themselves and to their own emotions. The recruitment of a team leader should include an assessment of their degree of empathy to others, in order to avoid future failures; this would save a lot of time and energy – and money – later on.

For a team leader, openness to others involves:

– letting go of stress, to not be in the grip of strong negative emotions and to be fully aware of their actions. This may require time and regular rest periods, or disconnection from the digital world. Cognitive abilities can only be improved;

– making themselves available to others, opening up their attention and listening skills and taking the time to talk to their teams, finding solutions together (in pairs or with several people) or calling on outside help. Employees then realize that they are being listened to and will participate all the better in the proposed project or action;

– knowing their own chronobiology and that of their team: adapting to different times is an important element in empathy;

– that the whole team is unified around the same objective, the completion of the project and its stages; the manager has an important role to play in this case.

To control the conversation, it is important to have a dialogue within a team: finding the right moment, knowing how to address the right person, focusing on the main point so as not to waste too much time, displaying listening skills and availability. Management by empathy often quite simply calls for common sense and humanity between people, which is something that today's society does not seem to favor or emphasize.

5.4. Change management (CM)

The transformation strategies mentioned above lead to modifications and changes in the processes or technical procedures: there may be changes within an organization, new rules to be implemented or a new service to be offered. This also applies to project management, which will be discussed later.

It is important to discuss change management theory: it refers to the approach that prepares and supports individuals, teams and organizations in achieving organizational change.

It includes:

– methods that redirect or redefine the use of resources;

– business processes;

– budgetary changes or other processes that significantly change a business or organization.

Change is a long-term process, which can cause resistance. Managing change in a structured and controlled manner is therefore essential to achieving the desired success. While all changes are unique and all individuals are unique, decades of research show that there are common measures that can help support people in their individual transitions. Change management provides a structured approach to helping people in the organization move from their current state to their future state.

– Questioning the importance of giving meaning to change.

– Having a global vision of the components of change: change as a process, the involvement of human and technical aspects.

– Understanding the keys to successful change.

– Implementing the different stages of change management.

– Identifying and defining the strategic focus and objectives within the environment and their impacts within the service or institution.

– Supporting and implementing change through a management style that is both structuring and participative.

Box 5.1. *A method for change management*

5.4.1. *The three levels of change management*

– Individual change management: requires an understanding of how change is experienced by individuals and what they need to make the change successful, as well as what will help people make the transition: what messages they need to hear; when and from whom; when is the right time to share a new skill with someone; how to get them to behave in a new way. Individual change management draws on disciplines such as psychology and neuroscience to apply frameworks to individual change.

– Organizational change management: involves identifying the groups and individuals impacted by the project and what will be required for them to accept the change. It involves creating a customized plan to ensure that affected employees are made aware of the change, with the guidance and training they need to make it work. Conducting successful transitions should be a central part of organizational change management activities.

– Enterprise change management capability: effective change management is embedded in the way the business operates, within the roles, structures, processes, projects and management skills of the organization. This is consistently and effectively applied to the initiatives undertaken.

5.5. Project management: theory and applications

Other management methods exist. We will explain them, in particular project management and agile methods in libraries.

What better way to explain a method than by way of an example? The decision was thus made to detail two experiments that I have conducted, here:

– the complete renovation of a library at the Faculty of Sciences at the University of Geneva[4];

---

[4] https://www.unige.ch/biblio/fr/infos/sites/sciences/; https://www.unige.ch/biblio/fr/infos/sites/sciences/.

– a project-based operation for the Library and Archives of the city of Lausanne[5] in Switzerland.

We will then return to some theoretical aspects of project management.

5.5.1. Project mode operation: two case studies

5.5.1.1. First case study: the library of the Faculty of Science, University of Geneva in Switzerland

The launch of a project such as the construction or renovation of a library is always a challenge for the person undertaking it, as well as for the teams involved: a challenge that is simultaneously professional and personal, architectural, cultural and often political.

This case refers to the renovation of an existing library at the Faculty of Sciences at the University of Geneva, located on the ground floor of the faculty, on the banks of a river – the Arve, a tributary of the Rhone – in the heart of the city of Geneva, in one of its popular and lively districts, little known to wealthy tourists and businessmen, the Jonction.

5.5.1.1.1. Negative and positive points: the reasons for the need to innovate

The current building (commonly known as Sciences 2) was representative of the architecture of the 1970s: concrete, steel and glass predominate, with, however, a significant presence of mahogany wood on large surfaces inside the building. The overall effect was one of gloom, and the atmosphere was dark, despite the building having bay windows.

As for the negative points, the old library did not escape this description, the lighting being a real weak point, a brown ceiling which, despite its height, felt oppressive, and the furniture was very solid, unattractive and dated, with only the shelves having been previously updated.

---

5 The author's experiences in 2009–2010 and 2012, respectively.

Although the floor had only been relaid a few years previously, it had a gray carpet that reinforced the idea of a sad place without real harmony. A reception desk, installed only five years previously[6], was located to the left of the main entrance, behind a pillar... thus demonstrating that welcoming users was not a priority. The librarians (about 10) were no better off, for the most part, sharing a large landscaped office furnished in a completely disparate manner and overlooking an inner courtyard. The collections (about 70,000 items) were stored on 10 parallel shelves in the central space of the library, reinforcing the notion of an archiving space, rather than a living place as a library can be.

On the positive side, attendance (mainly students and assistants, some professors and external readers) was good, with users occupying the 120 or so places available (including workstations and about 20 computer stations) in the 1,200 m^2 of the library (which makes it a medium-sized library) for fairly long periods of time. It should be noted, however, that this library (known as the "Central" library) federated a network of six other scientific libraries spread throughout the city of Geneva[7], which obviously multiplied the surface area and the number of available workspaces. With its imposing central platform, a main entrance on the ground floor of the faculty building with a separate secondary entrance at the back for weekend opening, the central library comprised two levels (lower and upper) on each side, with more spaces for quiet working, which was appreciated by students. This architecture, although overall very rectilinear, was nevertheless well suited to a library and explains why, in spite of everything, users frequented it. However, the faculty was aware that, after 40 years of existence, a renovation was necessary, if not imperative, and therefore launched a project approach, which was divided into major stages.

---

6 The reception was previously held in one of the librarians' offices.

7 In addition to the central library at Sciences 2, which is home to the Physics, Chemistry, Biology and Pharmaceutical Sciences sections, the network includes libraries of the following departments: Earth Sciences, Environment, Mathematics, Astronomy, Computer Science and Anthropology. See: http://www.unige.ch/biblio/sciences/infos.html.

5.5.1.1.2. The main stages of the renovation project
First stage: setting up the project group

The reflection on the renovation was initiated in 2008, before the arrival of the future project manager: the team of librarians participated in a consultation on the subject requested by the faculty administration, in order to see what corrections were possible, and a new distribution of tasks was also decided within the team.

This is one of the most interesting points of the project: a complete overhaul of the tasks in parallel with the future work[8]. Until March 2009, the Science Library, unlike the other faculty libraries[9], did not have its own management, but rather a coordinator. On March 1, 2009, a director was recruited, whose main mission was to carry out the project for the new library and to present it to a private foundation that had been funding the University of Geneva for many years, the Ernst and Lucie Schmidheiny Foundation[10], named after an old family from Swiss industry. The Faculty of Science, represented by its dean Jean-Marc Triscone, decided that the library was a priority project to be supported by the Foundation and the project manager was asked to set up a project group. In addition to the dean, the vice-dean in charge of the library and the faculty administrator, the group included the university's building managers, a member of the Swiss Library Service (a private company specializing in library furnishings and fittings[11]) and an architect: PlanungsBüro Chevalier, a consultancy firm with long-standing expertise in the field of libraries in Switzerland[12]. The choice of the signage designer came later, in the middle of the process.

---

8 However, this step is not addressed in this work.
9 There were – in 2009 – eight faculty libraries at the University of Geneva (in addition to the Sciences): Economic and Social Sciences, Psychology, Law, Medicine, Letters, Theology and Interfaculty Centers.
10 http://www.fondation-schmidheiny.ch/.
11 https://www.sbd.ch/fr/portrait_f/sbd_f/cooperation_avec_l_ekz.htm.
12 PlanungBüro Françoise Chevalier – Thun: contact chevalier.f@bluewin.ch.

Second stage: the project outline and acceptance by the Schmidheiny Foundation

Once in place, the project group met on average once a month: it had until the following May to put the project together. It was, of course, the broad outlines that were being decided upon, the architect being charged with responsibility for the general concept:

– the use of the original interior architecture, including the mahogany, concrete and steel; the whole interior was to be completely restored;

– the spaces were distributed differently: a modernized entrance door; a reception area identified and visible from the entrance; a different arrangement for the collections, divided into thematic zones, but in the same area as before; a training room equipped with computer stations; group work rooms for students; periodical collections archived using Compactus units and accessible to the public; reconfigured offices for the librarians;

– one constraint, however, was that there was to be no reduction in either the number of workplaces or the linear footage required for the collections and their development (the adjustment was therefore constant throughout the project);

– all interior furnishings were to be reviewed and renewed: false ceilings, carpeting, lighting, furniture and so on. Imposing cement pillars needed to be cleaned and sanded.

The general principle accepted by the project group was to truly offer users a comfortable, welcoming place to work and live, together with the latest technology. In addition, the three original sections (Pharmaceutical Sciences, Biology and Chemistry) had been joined by the Physics section, which meant that some 13,000 additional books and documents had to be recoded according to the Universal Decimal Classification (UDC) for integration into the general collection.

The Board of the Schmidheiny Foundation approved the project on May 26, 2009, in the presence of the rector of the University of Geneva, Mr. Jean-Dominique Vassalli, and the Dean of Science. A sum of 2 million Swiss francs was allocated for this project.

Third stage: first works, first disappointments

Since the issue of the collections and their growth – despite the significant arrival of digital technology in the sciences[13] – was crucial, two instances of Compactus (one in the basement, and the second directly accessible from one of the galleries) were installed, with the old ones destroyed from September to November 2009. Official authorization to proceed with the work was then granted all the more easily as the project would not involve breaking down any walls, or modifying the structure of the building itself. The first stage of the work was scheduled to take place from February to May 2010, leading to a partial closure of the library, followed by a second and final stage from July to September 2010, with a view to reopening for the start of the academic year. However, tests carried out in the water pipes indicated the presence of a tiny amount of asbestos in the insulation of the pipes, as was the practice in all buildings constructed at that time. The State of Geneva's security service demanded the closure of the premises, together with the removal of the collections, and, above all, the offices, with a view to completely removing asbestos from the premises. A temporary library was then set up on the first floor and operated from April to September 2010 with all services open to users, the book collections having been stored in the basement.

Fourth stage: the choices made by the architect and the project manager

In this type of project, the relationship of trust that is established between the appointed architect and the project manager is essential. In this case, this relationship was established very quickly, in view of the skills of the architect, who had significant experience both in libraries and project management.

First, the choices were discussed between the two protagonists, with full agreement, and then presented to the project group, with the final decision (in case of disputes) resting with the dean of the faculty.

---

13 This increase is currently for electronic journals, but books and monographs are still in paper format.

Colors and materials were examined; the distribution of collections and the delimitation of reception, work, office and consultation zones was decided upon, as well as the different types of furniture (such as tables, chairs, shelves and the reception desk). Very quickly, the appointment of a signage designer became necessary: the architect proposed the studio of Roger Pfund, a famous Swiss graphic designer known for having designed the Swiss banknotes and the recent giant portraits adorning the University of Geneva for its 450th anniversary[14]. The studio was then appointed to design a general signage concept, in line with that drawn up by the architect. This enabled the final choice of colors for the future Schmidheiny Library: gray on the floor with red stripes to delimit certain areas, the same red on the concrete pillars, display panels and on a map of the library and finally huge portraits of the founders, Mr and Mrs Schmidheiny, at the entrance. It is not always easy to make artists understand what a library really is, because they are more interested in esthetics than in practicality. However, little by little, through discussions and meetings, a visual identity for the future library was created, forming a definitive concept, approved by the entire project group. At the same time, the choice of furniture and lighting was made and orders were placed with suppliers, with regular adaptations (reductions or orders for additional furniture).

Fifth stage: resumption of work and reopening

In June 2010, the complete removal of asbestos from the library was completed and work could resume.

There was now a race against time, as everything had to be done during the summer months: the false ceiling had to be completely changed, the electricity and wiring had to be brought up to standard, the woodwork and steel frames had to be renovated, the floor and pillars had to be sanded and so on.

The building managers then had to mobilize the necessary companies, and weekly site meetings attended by the project manager became very useful for sorting out the multitude of outstanding

---

14 The Roger Pfund workshop no longer exists.

details, such as how to fill in such and such a space, how to replace such and such a panel damaged during the work and whether to move such and such an electrical socket.

Contacts with the architect, signage specialists and companies intensified as their work progressed. These were completed at the end of August 2010 and the furniture was delivered and installed, as well as the signage. The new library was reopened on September 20, the first day of the new academic year. The official inauguration took place on October 18, in the presence of officials, politicians and personalities from the Geneva and Swiss library community.

Summary

The result was a real success: the users were very satisfied, as were the librarians and the Faculty of Science as a whole[15]. The outcome is a harmonious site, bright and colorful without being overly so. This would not have been possible without the choice of competent partners and close cooperation between the architect, the signage specialists and the librarians. The Schmidheiny Foundation also actively participated in all the choices, which proved to be very important for the project itself: this made it possible to reduce certain financial items in order to give priority to others as choices and decisions were made.

Obviously, not everything was easy and some choices remain questionable (a carpeted floor, for example, when we know how difficult it is to keep the premises clean at the University); the follow-up of the work was not easy either, especially given the multitude of details to be resolved.

Understanding what a library is – a place to welcome and work, not to archive – for non-users required almost constant explanation to the different interlocutors. Librarians had also to be convinced of the importance of certain choices, while abandoning others. It therefore took much perseverance, power of conviction and diplomacy to ensure

---

15 The newsletter of the Swiss Library Service (which provides furniture to libraries) had for its 2010 news magazine, the headline "La Bibliothèque Schmidheiny à Genève : la perfection".

that all the pieces of the project would fit together properly. However, in the end, the result was compelling.

5.5.1.2. Second case study: libraries and archives of the city of Lausanne in Switzerland (Bibliothèques et Archives de la Ville de Lausanne, BAVL)[16]

In 2011, I was appointed to the Library and Archives Department of the City of Lausanne (BAVL) to assist management in defining their strategy and organizational chart, as well as in launching a number of projects. We will only consider here the strategy and projects aspect. BAVL has 70 employees, spread over a central site and five other sites in the city. After many turbulent years at the helm of the institution, the city of Lausanne decided to bring two entities (the municipal library and the city archives) together under a single management team. This made it possible to start again on a sounder footing, but the "strategy" aspect of the new entity remained to be defined. I then had the idea of resurrecting the structure established during my time at the University of Geneva, which had borne fruit, based on the "pillars of activity".

Following individual one-to-one interviews with each employee (over a period of three months), the needs emerged, including greater flexibility in the organization, a wealth of ideas for improving the library and archives and the importance of micro-projects.

The activity pillars provided a clear picture of all the activities carried out within the new entity. The new organization chart was based on these activities, and each employee could find their place within it. In order to avoid too much hierarchy, it was then decided to add a cross-sectional base entitled "cross-sectional projects" to the activity pillars: this meant that the combination of "activities and projects" allowed each employee of the institution (storekeeper, employee or manager) to propose a project of any kind (micro-project or interdepartmental) and to submit a request. When the proposal was accepted, a project manager would be appointed, designating a project

---

16 For reasons of confidentiality, the author can only give a few elements to illustrate the case study.

group composed of people from different departments. Training in the project approach was organized for managers and management.

This new global approach was then presented to all the teams, and about 20 projects of all kinds were submitted in 2012–2013.

6

Some Theory on Management and Leadership

The experiences and case studies previously discussed provide some possible learnings on management and leadership. The proximity between managers and their teams is very important, even essential[1]: knowing everyone's tasks, encouraging initiative, showing confidence are essential principles for success. The manager's role is usually one of close supervision (advisor, decision-maker, assessor), which may vary according to the activity prescribed. Overall, managers assign certain team members to more specific tasks and set procedures (task rotation).

The manager corrects errors and shortcomings, without waiting for repetition to lead to damaging habits. It could be said that they provide production management of the service through their role as facilitator, their technical knowledge and their professional competence.

Proximity allows for a different kind of communication with teams, which therefore encourages cohesion, provided that those teams are involved in the ongoing projects and, in a best case scenario, are regularly kept informed. Leaving room to maneuver, and taking individual initiatives, stems from such an attitude. This is the best way to create the trust that is so necessary between a manager and their

---

1 This proximity is obviously easier in smaller teams (one to five people).

team: trust cannot be acquired without these elements, which are, after all, complex to build and require time and perseverance.

Communication therefore plays an essential role: regular agenda-based team meetings make it possible to transmit the information necessary for the team to function and to report on various activities, such as incidents. They are quick, prepared in advance and effective, so should not be confused with meetings to work on a specific activity or with project meetings. Consultation and participation in projects are the reference values and form the subject of minutes to which it is possible to refer. This is part of formal communication. Informal communication within the team takes place during external visits, meetings, shared meals and conversations and is at least as important as formal communication.

6.1. New management methods: Design Thinking, user experience and agile methods

Three innovative approaches – which may work in competition or in complementarity – are developed here:

– Design Thinking;

– user experience;

– agile methods.

Design Thinking and user experience have already been applied in libraries with some success. Several well-known information professionals have been promoting these approaches to good effect: training courses, study days, courses and various articles (in journals or blogs) have made this possible. They appear to be flexible and adaptable to different contexts, while focusing on user guidance. There are also some very useful advantages to agile methods, which are more structured, and they are therefore explained below.

6.1.1. *Design Thinking*

New trends are appearing in the world of libraries, and most often they have been tried out in other fields: to marketing, economics and business, we can now add the world of design. Indeed, the product creators (who design the products we consume, as well as their packaging and logos) adopt a very concrete method of problem solving, in contrast with the dominant practices which still favor the final product. Designers propose several prototypes that are eliminated or improved over time, until one becomes the final product. This is a practical method that is increasingly being used in libraries.

6.1.1.1. *Defining Design Thinking*

How do we define Design Thinking? It is a method of brainstorming and prototyping to solve a problem: several ideas are proposed and tested one after another until the best solution is found. The Nueva School in California[2] has adopted a fairly explicit model, which shows that cooperation between individuals and the specific aspect are central to the concept. First, the protagonists – in this case, the students of the Nueva School – are faced with a problem and carry out research in order to better understand it. They will observe, ask questions and look for broad responses. Second, they define the problems and synthesize their findings, in order to see what they need to resolve.

The next step is brainstorming: ideas for solutions are proposed by the whole group without any particular sorting, the point being to generate the maximum number of ideas possible. They then select the solutions that seem most feasible, create object or service prototypes and, above all, submit them to the others. They then collect the opinions of the group to improve their creations.

In professional environments, it is at this stage that representatives of the end users appear to give their opinion. Eventually, the different groups will pool their solutions. The principle is not to be the best, but

---

2 https://www.nuevaschool.org/.

to cooperatively work to propose the best products and services. This method of working is transversal and brings together several disciplines or values.

This theory, which is now applied in many fields, is not, in fact, new. As early as the 1950s, the theory of brainstorming was born from the imagination of Alex Osborn[3] and "creative thinking" was developed, highlighting the richness of shared ideas: creative thinking is defined as "the ability to think in a particular and original way. It involves thinking outside the box in order to come up with alternative and authentic solutions"[4]. The theory of Design Thinking was then successfully taken up in the 2000s by David M. Kelley and Tim Brown[5] and adopted with no little success by the GAFAM companies[6]; the rest is history. The education and teaching communities then appropriated this method, which has become central to the educational process in some establishments, as learning is greatly improved compared to more traditional methods, such as courses given *ex cathedra*, which do not invite the participation of students. Not to be outdone, some universities want to attract young creatives into their ranks. Libraries have understood – or are beginning to integrate – the benefits of this method.

6.1.1.2. *Design Thinking applied to libraries*[7]

As Nicolas Beudon indicated in an interview with *Doc pour docs*[8], this method is not fundamentally new or original, but it should be understood by information professionals:

---

3 Alex Osborn is an American advertising executive. To learn more about brainstorming theory: https://www.lescahiersdelinnovation.com/2015/08/le-brainstorming/.
4 Delécraz, J. (2016). La pensée créative, qu'est-ce que c'est ? *Blog CogniFit* [Online]. Available at: https://blog.cognifit.com/fr/pensee-creative/.
5 https://fr.wikipedia.org/wiki/IDEO_(design).
6 Acronym formed by the initial letter of the five companies Google, Apple, Facebook, Amazon and Microsoft.
7 IDEO (2016). Le Design thinking en bibliothèque [Online]. Available at: http://lrf-blog.com/wp-content/uploads/2016/01/DTEB-Guide-methodologique-2016.pdf.
8 https://www.docpourdocs.fr/spip.php?article614.

What design thinking brings is a precise methodology that allows us to act on the conviction that the user is important. There are very simple tools that allow us to identify unsatisfied needs, represent experiences or to produce new ideas in a collaborative way[9].

When this method is applied more specifically to the world of libraries, it enables the design of services based on the experience and expectations of users. Problems can thus be solved differently, using empathy, observation and experimentation: decisions will be made according to what the user actually wants. Traditional project management and management methods are therefore not involved: space is left for a process of joint creativity. Design Thinking is characterized by three phases:

– inspiration: understanding needs, creating a public dialogue and observing;

– ideation: generating ideas and creating prototypes;

– iteration: testing prototypes with users.

Some projects, such as the BiblioRemix or the Hackathon of the Bibliothèque nationale de France (BnF), were inspired by Design Thinking.

6.1.2. *User experience*

"User experience" (UX) puts the user at the heart of all types of activities: primarily commercial, of course, as well as in cultural institutions, health care and public services in general. The UX approach has been developed over the last 20 years and is changing the face of institutions that have adopted it. Some people call this transformation a user empowerment, but is it not, rather, a fair rebalancing, as users are best able to judge a product or a service that they are using, even more so than the person who created or

---

9 Beudon, N. (2017). *Docs pour docs*.

developed it? This aspect therefore concerns libraries and information services, which have been adopting it for several years (even without realizing).

The idea behind UX is to stay connected and to maintain a strong relationship with users by using conversation, in other words, by opening up interaction on networks. This is one of the basic principles of the new economy which, if not adopted in traditional and service economies, is likely to lead to a loss of real contact with users. "The customer is king" is the new motto: taken in a purely commercial sense; this may put librarians off, but, in a broader sense, it is synonymous with the motto used in this chapter: the user at the heart.

Conversely, there are a number of factors that can trigger a poor user experience. These include:

– being ignored;

– being left out;

– suffering from red tape;

– being confronted with incompetence;

– being in a situation where no one takes responsibility;

– feeling powerless;

– not being respected.

In these different cases, this means that users are able to give their opinion, positive or negative, to make recommendations and to converse with professionals – in short, to participate in the life of the product or service.

Through the use of these recommender systems – as well as other types of reviews and "likes" – we can say that users have a certain power and have tamed the Web.

> Users of online bookstores, such as Amazon or Fnac, are familiar with recommendation systems, with the phrase that usually follows the consultation of a book: "Other users also bought...". An algorithm can cross-reference similar choices from potential buyers and propose them to others. Recommendations are also used by researchers in the scientific field (saving time, which is useful for research).
>
> Recommendation systems are seen as an extension of library catalogues and as a replacement for subject classifications. In the area of information dissemination, they are useful:
>
> – for the researcher, in the advancement of the research;
>
> – for the library, to build user loyalty through a loyalty system and system of notifications;
>
> – for authors, allowing them to find articles similar to their work;
>
> – for publishers, similar works or authors in their catalogue.
>
> Library-related recommender systems include: BibTip at the University of Karlsruhe, xLibris bx, FoxTrot, LIBRA (Learning Intelligent Book Recommending Agent) and OCLC Kindred.

Box 6.1. *Recommender systems*

6.2. User power

With the tools made available (mobile apps were downloaded more than 27 billion times in the first quarter of 2018[10]), users are able to act and interact constantly and continuously; they can instantly search for any type of subject or product. In the 1970s, a company had to find customers for its products and the very essence of marketing, the main lever of this, was sustained visibility: be seen, be loved, be chosen. Today's slogan is "be found, be shared and stay connected". For the user, what is important is their experiences with these uses.

---

10 https://www.generation-nt.com/record-27-5-milliards-applications-telechargees-premier-trimestre-2018-actualite-1952747.html.

Brand loyalty becomes paramount[11] – this is true in all areas: travel, leisure, reading, purchasing goods and so on – and generates an experience that is intended to be unique. Multiple brands are usually involved in the user experience. Mobility accentuates this effect, especially in relation to companies that offer travel services, such as SNCF, Blablacar and Booking.com. They not only offer fares and destinations, but, above all, life experiences that will then be discussed and shared.

Seth Godin, American author and speaker, states:

> Delivering fluid, comfortable experiences to your customers is much more powerful than trying to find customers for your products[12].

The experience (of buying, traveling or reading) is therefore as important as the product itself, leading to user recognition. Implicitly, the desired effect is to create loyalty to one or more brands[13]. Loyalty implies that the satisfied user shares their satisfaction within their (mostly virtual) community.

All the elements described above are fully applicable to libraries, which are similar, more or less, to certain cultural industries and have something to offer the user: they offer an experience, a place, a welcome and content. Online they, too, create virtual communities of users through networks. While their brand image tends to improve and be more anchored in today's reality, there is still some work to be done for better visibility and greater personalization.

6.3. Setting up and managing an agile project[14]

Agility in project management refers to flexible and mobile working methods. Dating back to the late 1990s, agile methods

---

11 See Part 4.
12 Godin, S. (2018). Siècle digital [Online]. Available from: https://siecledigital.fr/2018/10/04/user-experience-at-new-business/.
13 See Part 4 and Chapter 12 on branding.
14 This section is inspired by: Scalla, A. (2018). Les Méthodes agiles et les bibliothèques. Dissertation, Enssib Lyon.

constitute a framework for activity, with a view to carrying out and managing projects, while overcoming certain obstacles – administrative burden, team reticence, communication problems – relating to more traditional management methods. This method was first adopted in IT and, more particularly, in software development.

6.3.1. *The application of agile methods*

Originating from the business world, agile methods are being applied in digital projects of public services, which is why they interest us in relation to libraries. A recent report by the French *Cour des Comptes* even sees this type of approach as a way to avoid overly ambitious projects that often lead to failure:

> This is the case for the diffusion of the so-called agile method in the ministries: this term describes the will to act in a flexible, reactive and rapid manner, avoiding systemic approaches and taking into account the opinion of users at each stage of the production process. So there is a real change in the approach and handling of digital projects[15].

The scrum (taken from the rugby term for a melée) is the agile method typically used today. Rather than a method, it is more a state of mind involving the whole team over a period of time (a few months) and working in a transversal and not vertical relationship mode. We can, however, cite some obstacles in the library context to the culture of agility:

– the use of an essentially Anglophone vocabulary that is not widely accepted by French professionals, as it is considered too fashionable or part of the corporate world;

– fixed and calibrated work sessions, which appear to be restrictive;

---

15 2016 report from the *Cour des Comptes*, "Rapport d'information sur l'évaluation de la modernisation numérique de l'État".

– interactive sessions, using less traditional animation methods such as games, role-playing and speaking.

These obstacles are obviously not found everywhere, but are a reflection of library culture, where each role has its own habits and customs. Promoters of the agile method therefore emphasize the need to regularly explain the progress and development of projects.

6.3.2. *Agility in libraries*

Agility is defined as a set of work practices and professional relationships that are both flexible and vertical (and therefore less hierarchical).

The term "flexibility" is becoming synonymous with agility and with finding alternative ways of working together as a team. Working sessions are short (30 minutes maximum), more dynamic, focused on the exchange of information and interactive; they are daily or weekly and may involve two or more team members.

In her dissertation[16], Anaïs Scalla discusses three institutions in France that are experimenting with the agile method, mainly for IT projects: the *Bibliothèque nationale de France* (BnF), for the digital legal deposit, for instance, the *Institut national de l'Information Scientifique et Technique* (Inist) and the *Archives Nationales*. It is immediately apparent that these are large institutions in terms of size, budget and staff. Of course, they certainly have the necessary resources, a culture of agility and a record of managing large-scale projects. However, they also use other complementary project methods.

There are different ways to use the agile method, possibly within a larger project involving several methods, applied simply to the project team or linked with a non-agile project. Scalla cites the example of the *Archives Nationales*:

---

16 Scalla, A. (2018). Les Méthodes agiles et les bibliothèques. Dissertation, Enssib, Lyon.

The project conducted using so-called "flexible" project management for the redesign of the Virtual Inventory Room (*Salle des Inventaires Virtuelle*, SIV) aims to improve the search catalogue by working in particular on the relevance of results, the ergonomics of the service and new search assistance tools. This project is an evolution of the existing Archival Information System (*Système d'Information Archivistique*, SIA). However, the SIA will undergo transformations in connection with another Adamant[17] project, conducted in agile mode, which will develop the electronic archive system.

Other configurations exist, such as large agile projects that are made up of agile sub-projects.

6.4. Library management and leadership, constantly redefined concepts

In one of his most famous books[18], Henry Mintzberg, one of the champions of management theory, explains the activities of the manager, grouped according to four main headings:

– regarding the outside world: spokesperson, figurehead for the managed entity (service, office, department and so on), link between the entity and various environments;

– regarding information: disseminator, relay, active sensor;

– regarding decision-making: allocating resources according to the preferred objectives;

– regarding people: leader, facilitator, counsellor, trainer, evaluator[19].

---

17 Archives Nationales (2019). Adamant : projet d'avenir [Online]. Available at: http://www.archives-nationales.culture.gouv.fr/web/guest/archiver-les-donnees-numeriques-adamant [Accessed June 12, 2019].
18 Minzberg, H. (1984). *Le Manager au quotidien*. Éditions d'Organisation, Paris.
19 *Ibid.*

Thus, the manager and leader fulfil multiple roles, which evolve with time and economic contexts, as well as cultural and social ones. In view of what has just been described above, it seems difficult, even unworkable, to be a leader or team leader in the same way as 20 or 30 years ago.

The relationship between the manager and their team has various aspects. Two management schools are in conflict, directive management and participatory management, which we support because it is more flexible. It takes into account the skills and abilities of each person, enables delegation and is based on trust.

The department manager is part of the management hierarchy and is accountable to a director. Similarly, team members are accountable to the department manager. They cannot work without the mediation of their manager, who proposes the department's policy and obtains the means to implement it from management. However, the smooth running of the department depends on the goodwill of each individual. A close interdependence is established and responsibility towards management and staff is therefore assumed, thanks to constant mediation which must be exercised with firmness, flexibility and diplomacy[20].

---

20 Section inspired by: Accart, J.-P. and Réthy, M.-P. (eds) (2015). Part 2 : Le métier. In *Le Métier de documentaliste*. Editions du Cercle de La Librairie, Paris.

PART 3

Library Tools and Technology

7

The Digital Transformation of Libraries

The global trend in information technology today is to adopt the principles of uniqueness and interoperability between heterogeneous functions or software, the latter involving multiple accesses to information, making its distribution more complex. With the use of some of these global offerings – as is already the case – it is possible to imagine the library as a service and no longer as an administrative entity or an institution. There is greater flexibility and increased visibility once users understand its purpose. Obviously, this does not mean the end of the library space as discussed in Part 1, but it is completed and enriched by the digital space.

While the library is generally seen as an institution, it can also be seen as a service in its own right. The service concept contains several elements. Service is a polysemous term which, when applied to a library, a documentation service or an archive, implies several notions:

– those of public service, service offer, service obligation and service rendered. The library encompasses all these concepts. With the introduction of marketing in the library world, the notion of "client" or "customer" has gradually become established, but we prefer the notion of "user";

– working in a library is a service profession since it essentially depends on the user's request and the response provided;

– the notion of service takes on its full meaning insofar as users actively participate in its production: through their requests, through the information they hold, they contribute essential elements to the final result. We can then speak of coproduction, insofar as the service is coproduced by its user: the organization of this service is considered as a whole, bringing together the library system (the infrastructure) and the service production system (the servuction). A service relationship is established with the user.

In addition to the general concept of service, the concept of digital or online service is increasingly emerging at present. It is not possible to think about a service package without including online services: these are, then, part of a service policy.

7.1. The library as a service: from catalogues to digital platforms

Among the platforms we will review in this chapter are:

– Platform as a Service (PaaS);

– library intranets, information and library portals, repositories and digital libraries;

– library service platforms;

– monitoring, economic intelligence and curation platforms;

– social platforms;

– open access platforms for archiving documents and data.

7.1.1. *Service platforms*

7.1.1.1. *Generalist platforms*

There are several types of service platforms, most notably those based on cloud computing:

– IaaS (Infrastructure as a Service): the operating system and applications are installed by clients on servers to which they connect as on a conventional computer;

– PaaS (Platform as a Service): the cloud service provider administers the operating system and its tools. The customer can install their own applications;

– SaaS (Software as a Service): applications are provided in the form of turnkey services to which users connect with a dedicated software or a web browser. For the general public, these are, for example, electronic messaging systems such as Gmail, Yahoo, Outlook or office suites such as Office 365 or the Google app.

It should be noted that PaaS is currently the system most widely used by libraries.

Take the example of Slack[1], which is a collaboration platform launched in 2015 that enables work, links and conversations from many other applications to be aggregated on a single tool: employees follow the progress of different projects in a less fragmented way and it reduces email overload.

Messages and files from about 30 different sources, such as Twitter, Dropbox, Google Drive, Asana, GitHub, Zendesk and Mail Chimp, as well as various instant messages, are collected and available from this single access point. Announcements, alerts, follow-ups and other data in a communication stream are integrated, where and when appropriate. Slack allows both trivial and important information to be shared through the creation of dedicated channels or groups. Teams can create open channels for projects, groups and topics and set up custom notifications. Work in progress can be viewed on a dashboard.

Slack is a tool used daily by each member of a work team, with different tools available, to build their projects together and without constraint. Slack also has a search function and a document transfer

---

1 https://slack.com/.

tool. The system analyzes all these functions and provides reports on usage statistics. It offers free usage for small-scale users, followed by a cost of $8 or $15 per month per user, depending on storage needs. In addition to these various aspects, it addresses the problem of the profusion of multiple modes of communication, by grouping together as many applications as possible and streamlining digital uses and sources of information.

According to a recent analysis by *Journal du Net*, the use of PaaS technology is growing at an annual rate of 25%.

PaaS architecture simplifies the deployment of software, enabling better results, both economically and in terms of staff management and the dissemination of information.

Four benefits are highlighted:

– Speed: developers are spared the steps of configuring the cloud technology and the transition to it is therefore faster, as the infrastructure is already operational. PaaS services are preconfigured, instantly available and processes are automated. The IT environment is thus made more coherent.

– Experimentation: infrastructure automation enabled by PaaS helps us to better control development costs. Teams are able to experiment and test applications and get results directly. The appropriation of the tool by individuals is easier.

– Flexibility: not all applications lend themselves to operation in the public cloud, as security and regulatory compliance constraints are imposed on companies in many sectors. However, an application developed using PaaS can be deployed in any type of infrastructure: dedicated server, cloud or hosting site. If the infrastructure changes, it is always possible to move the application, hence its flexibility.

– Cost: many PaaS solutions are open source, which allows for better cost management, compared with proprietary software. PaaS is often a key component of Big Data analytics solutions, with many companies specifically adopting it for their Big Data projects[2].

> Big Data refers to the large volumes of computer data that are considered the raw material of tomorrow. The "Big Data phenomenon", according to Viktor Mayer-Schönberger, professor of Internet governance at Oxford University, refers to the ability "to draw conclusions from a large amount of data that we could not draw from a smaller amount". This is particularly true in the stock market and financial sector: on Wall Street, billions of decisions can be made in one second. Google is also a good example: on the right-hand side of the homepage, you can see paid advertisements and, at the top, sponsored links. These advertising spaces are auctioned in real time, depending on the nature of the user's search. Google then makes a bid on the market which is evaluated by other algorithms, which then determines whether that space should be bought or not. This process happens 40 or 50 billion times a day for Google alone.

Box 7.1. *Big Data*

7.1.1.2. *Library service platforms*

These are integrative platforms dedicated to library services and include generalist, monitoring and curation and open archive platforms. Three examples of major library service platforms using cloud computing technologies are: WorldShare, from Online Computer Library Center (OCLC); EBSCO Integrated Library System (ILS), from the EBSCO corporation; Alma, from Ex-Libris Group. They are designed for professional use, but, of course, have applications for users.

– OCLC[3] WorldShare provides a comprehensive set of library management applications and services from a cloud computing platform. Like the WorldCat[4] catalog, which integrates centralized resources for library data, WorldShare provides a centralized platform of services for libraries to manage their operations, service offerings

---

2 See Box 7.4.
3 https://www.oclc.org/fr/worldshare.html.
4 https://www.worldcat.org/.

and workflows. Management tasks are consolidated into a single platform, integrating applications developed by OCLC and other library service providers. These tasks include acquisitions, circulation, metadata management, resource sharing, discovery, reporting and license management.

– EBSCO Integrated Library System (ILS)[5] is a user-oriented platform that aims to help manage digital content in addition to print. The focus is on the interoperability of the ILS system proposed, that is, the ability of a product or system, whose interfaces are fully known, to work with other existing or future products or systems without restrictions on access or implementation. Adoption of the ILS solution requires prior consideration of:

- the user interface;

- the contents to be taken into account (full text, databases, e-books, images, videos);

- the ability to adapt the solution to specific research needs;

- the ability to interact with the ILS solution.

– Alma, from Ex-Libris[6], is currently very popular in the ILS market. It has the same characteristics as the two previous platforms with respect to the integration of library functionalities and cloud computing. Alma's design addresses the need to unify disparate or heterogeneous systems. Several hundred libraries worldwide are equipped with Ex-Libris. This ILS solution, which appears to be very complete and reliable, is of interest to large academic institutions, such as the Swiss Library Service Platform (SLSP) project.

> The Swiss Library Service Platform (SLSP) project is part of the swissuniversities "Scientific Information: Access, Processing and Storage" program[7].

---

5 https://connect.ebsco.com/s/article/EBSCO-ILS-Linking-Initiatives?language=en_US.
6 https://www.exlibrisgroup.com/fr/produits/alma/.
7 https://www.swissuniversities.ch/.

> SLSP is a national platform for scientific libraries based in Switzerland. It is based on a new generation, centralized library management system, the application of uniform norms and standards and an appropriate governance and organizational structure.
>
> This vision is delivered in three phases, the first phase dealing with the design (2015–2017), and the second and third phases the development of the organization and the realization of the platform with the development of a basic service offer (2017–2020), respectively.
>
> The project involves scientific libraries, as well as representatives of networks and universities from the German-, French- and Italian-speaking parts of Switzerland.
>
> All Swiss university libraries, or the networks to which they belong, are now faced with two challenges: on the one hand, it is essential to renew the IT solutions currently in use and to adapt them to the state of the art; on the other hand, this need offers a formidable opportunity to fundamentally reshape the Swiss library landscape. At present, libraries and their customers use different network catalogues, which leads to redundant library work and a sub-optimal service for users. The implementation of SLSP will enable routine tasks and mass processing to be pooled and, at least in principle, to ensure that they are carried out largely centrally. The area that should benefit most from this development is that of digital resources. With the planned integration of the Swiss University Library Consortium into SLSP, these resources can also be administered centrally, thus optimizing their use.

Box 7.2. *The Swiss Library Service Platform (SLSP) project*[8]

7.1.2. *Library intranets, information portals and digital repositories*

Along with the need to develop new skills, the digital environment is leading to a significant structural change.

---

8 www.slsp.ch.

The past few years have seen the combined effect of a number of factors, including:

– the deployment of complex IT architectures and information networks;

– the implementation of governmental and European programs to increase the use of digital technology by citizens;

– the creation of digital resource centers (schools, universities, legal, scientific, technical and so on).

In the public sector, this structural evolution is reflected in the emergence of entirely digital information architectures (such as Gallica, service-public.fr, legifrance.fr, thematic digital universities and Canal-U) that combine up-to-date digital content with digital services.

The commercial sector is not left behind – and is often ahead of the public sector – with YouTube, Instagram, Flickr, Google Books and others.

These architectures now take the form of repositories or digital libraries, and constitute document systems. One of the forms which predated these systems (but which still exists) is the library intranet, which uses Internet technology for internal use only and is generally an integral part of the company's or institution's intranet site, with pages dedicated to document services and products. It can be either an information or document portal. Portals are sites that provide access to a set of resources and services, either based on a theme, aimed at a specific audience or linked to an organization. They are similar to collaborative platforms, but these are more oriented towards e-learning.

However, the information portal is an elaborate and relatively mature form of service platform, which can be improved upon.

Both public and academic libraries are developing information portals as a privileged access point for users. They may contain services such as:

– simultaneous querying of databases or federated search: a federated search engine is a search tool that provides the user with a single search form, then transmits the query to different remote databases, retrieves the list of their results and displays it on a single page for the user;

– the catalogue of the Bibliothèque Municipale de Lyon (BML), *Catalog +*, is constructed according to this philosophy[9]. A survey conducted by the Rennes Regional Training Unit for Scientific and Technical Information (*Unité Régionale de Formation à l'Information Scientifique et Technique*, URFIST) indicates that, when searching for information, portals are used by 53% of the PhD student population (93% for search engines). In many cases, the federated search engine is supplanted by a discovery tool, which simplifies the search and is based on the same principle;

– online applications: forms for interlibrary loans, contacts, document reservations and so on;

– tools for students including course materials, exercises, online tutorials (e-learning): in the academic world, the best known platforms are the LMS (Learning Management System) and Moodle;

– management of the user profile with personalization of the services offered, the use of a password;

– other functionalities can be added, in order to make online mediation more effective:

- an integrated search engine, with visual facet,

- a chat to directly interact with users,

- a specific design of the pages and the portal,

- administration of online communities,

---

9 https://catalogue.bm-lyon.fr/.

- a system of recommendations,

- the presentation of thematic universes,

- a link to library software, for the management of references,

- one or more blogs,

- a link to social networks or RSS feeds,

- one or more avatars.

– Digital universities portal: http://www.france-universite-numerique.fr.

– French law portal: http://www.droit.org.

– French contemporary music portal: http://www.musiquecontemporaine.fr.

– Lille media libraries portal: http://portail.bibliotheque.bm-lille.fr.

– Lectura, the Rhône-Alpes portal of libraries: http://www.lectura.fr.

– Persée, Journals on humanities and social sciences: http://www.persee.fr.

– European archives portal: https://www.archivesportaleurope.net.

– Online archives: http://www.archives-online.org.

Box 7.3. *Some examples of information portals*

7.1.3. *Monitoring, business intelligence and curation platforms*

By the very nature of monitoring and business intelligence, which consists of surveying the environment (such as economic, technological, political, military and health), it is necessary to create tools that can monitor multiple objects, such as trends, publications, gray literature and statistics. The software solutions developed are therefore similar to document service platforms because they aggregate heterogeneous content to deliver an automatic or partial synthesis, which can then be analyzed by monitoring and curation professionals. SerdaLAB regularly publishes studies on the subject[10].

Significant examples of monitoring platforms[11] include:

– Arisem, a legacy company in the business intelligence sector (a subsidiary of the Thales group), offers the Kaliwatch Information Miner 2 strategic intelligence platform[12].

– Digimind[13] is a leading provider of strategic intelligence and image monitoring solutions to a large number of major accounts, including many CAC 40 companies. It is characterized by a constant innovation.

– AMI Software, with its AMI Enterprise Intelligence[14] software, is a solution for monitoring and capitalizing on knowledge, including online information collection, processing of collected information, capitalization of documents and sharing of comments.

– Copernic, with Copernic Agent Professional, also includes monitoring functionalities: monitoring of web pages and searches queried through the engine. Today, it is particularly the Copernic Desktop Search solution[15] that stands out.

Data curation is closely associated with intelligence. The term has been in use for some time and seems to be an avenue for documentalists and librarians to explore. The term "curation" was first quoted in 2008–2009 and originated in English-speaking countries: a

---

10 http://www.serdalab.com.
11 Among the paid platforms: AMI Software, Arisem, Digimind, Iscope, Ixxo, KB Crawl, Knowings, Lexis Nexis Analytics, Lingway, Neotia, Qwam, SindUp, Spotter and Trendy Buzz. There are free monitoring platforms, such as Netvibes or Feedly. RSS feeds are included in this category.
12 http://www.kaliwatch.com/.
13 https://www.digimind.com/fr/.
14 https://portail-ie.fr/resource/outils/604/solutions-ami.
15 http://www.copernic.com/fr/products/desktop-search/.

curator is a person who selects works of art for an exhibition, according to a certain type of audience; a content curator is therefore a person who shares their digital discoveries on the Internet on sites such as Delicious, Scoop.it, Pearltrees and Pinterest. However, what do we really mean by curation? According to Véronique Mesguich:

> Curation consists of identifying a variety of digital content according to a given theme, selecting and filtering the most relevant, organizing and structuring it through a scenography device and promoting its distribution[16].

Rohit Bhargava, an online digital marketing specialist, offers five curation templates:

– aggregation of sources;

– distillation, taking the essential elements from the sources;

– elevation, which allows trends to be identified from partial data;

– mashup, a technique that juxtaposes and merges content;

– ante-chronological organization (most recent to oldest).

In reality, many documentalists and librarians create their own curation spaces with new content, using learned library techniques; they communicate about it and disseminate the information to targeted communities. They maintain a thesaurus or repository, using formats such as the Resource Description Framework (RDF), and ensure that archival data and publications can be linked, with a focus on structured data. The Isidore platform[17], the primary platform for

---

16 Mesguich, V., Pierre, J., Alloing, C., Gallezot, G., Serres, A., Peirano, R., Frossard, F., Deschamps, C., Battisti, M., Martinet, F. (2012). Enjeux et dimensions. *Documentaliste-Science de l'information*, 49, 24–45.

17 https://isidore.science/.

enrichment and access to Open Data and documents in the humanities and social sciences, is a good example of this.

Regarding content curation platforms[18], the most used and popular are becoming monitoring platforms. For instance:

– Scoop.it, a practical online tool to set up and share a reactive information watch using selected keywords;

– Paper.li, offers the regular publication of a newspaper based on content from direct curation or from social networks;

– Pinterest, for image-centric curation;

– Storify aggregates content found on the Web (such as photos, videos, sounds and tweets). This allows the user to tell and shape a real story, offering a kind of storyboard;

– Pearltrees creates mind maps composed of pearls, in other words, useful resources from the Web. This tool organizes curation in an intelligent way;

– Flipboard is the curation tool for mobile devices, tablets and smartphones. Its magazine-like interface makes it easy to use.

7.1.4. *Social platforms*

7.1.4.1. *Generalist social networks*

Social platforms are very different in their approach, but complement the platforms outlined above and are useful and even essential for the supply and distribution of information, monitoring and curation. They are one of the elements in the digital presence of an individual or an entity[19]. In terms of mediation, they are used here as examples of how exchanges and interactions can take place within

---

18 http://outilsveille.com/2013/11/15-outils-de-curation-incontournables/.
19 See Chapter 11.

a community. The other platforms mentioned also offer interactions, but with a different impact and purpose.

However, the question is: which social platform should the library choose? Facebook, Twitter, YouTube, Pinterest, Instagram... There are tens, even hundreds, of social media platforms available, and these are only the most general ones. The selection is vast and the choice of which network to use depends on the resources available to the library (especially in relation to the staff who are in charge of these media and who monitor them on a daily basis) and on the institution's communication policy.

Nowadays, it seems hard to ignore social media and its impact on all types of audiences. It is these media, with the exception of institutional web pages, that are really shaping a digital presence on the Internet, through the construction of a brand[20], a specific design and a marketing approach that is different from that used for other services.

The Facebook platform appears to be a logical choice, as it is the most popular platform, with the largest audience, used by all age groups. However, its incredible popularity can have negative sides (in relation to online reputation, for example, or the capturing of personal data). It may be necessary for the library to diversify its choices by selecting other platforms. It is then necessary to define a media plan.

7.1.4.2. *Social network analysis*

This section provides the essential keys to understanding the particularities of each of these platforms. They are analyzed according to four criteria:

– referencing;

– exposure;

---

20 See Chapter 12.

– customer relations;

– online traffic generation.

The following is a summary of several major social media platforms: Twitter, Facebook, LinkedIn, YouTube, Pinterest and Instagram:

– Twitter is a recommended microblogging platform according to the four criteria mentioned above. Profiles are starting to be well referenced, traffic is high and the various publishing tools (notably the scheduling and automation functions) ensure a high level of visibility, which can be improved with sponsored content offers. Internet users are becoming accustomed to this means of communication, to challenge or be challenged by a brand. A downside to this analysis is that the Twitter audience in France is not truly representative of the population, with the elites being more active on the platform than the general public.

– Facebook is the most used platform, generating the most incoming traffic; however, the referencing of content is very limited. It offers great flexibility in the applications that can be linked to a page (through tabs) and especially offers a targeted (paid) advertising engine.

– LinkedIn is the social platform of reference for everything related to work and the professional world. It seems that recruiters are increasingly using this platform to select potential candidates for a job. It is therefore worthwhile for users to take care in how they express their personal profiles. In this context, the interest of LinkedIn lies in the possibility of participating in specialized groups that function as forums for exchange. The sharing site SlideShare (for slide presentations and online courses) is part of the LinkedIn group.

– YouTube is the most popular video hosting and sharing platform. It claims to be the second-most popular search engine after Google and has a global audience. It is possible to create a TV channel and to feed this channel with reports or short films.

– Pinterest is the most popular inspiration site, benefiting from very good referencing and generating highly qualified traffic for brands that know how to exploit it in a smart way. However, interaction with members is rather poor, even non-existent.

– Instagram is the most popular photo-sharing application for major brands. However, usage is mainly concentrated on mobile devices and the impact on referencing is almost zero. However, this application offers interesting possibilities with the introduction of videos and private messages.

In the context of this short section, we should also mention social media such as Tumblr, Snapchat, TikTok and mobile applications or also conversational platforms like Reddit (a community bookmarking website that allows users to submit their links and vote for links proposed by other users) or Quora (an online question/answer platform)[21].

7.1.4.3. *Social networks and libraries*

Several library experiments are taking place:

– the association Bibliothèques Sans Frontières[22] (BSF) has launched BSF Education, a learning channel on YouTube, to answer questions from schoolchildren on topics such as secularism, freedom of expression and conscience, racism, antisemitism, xenophobia and blasphemy;

– the Bibliothèques Municipales de Genève (Geneva Public Libraries) have their own YouTube channel[23], which presents new releases and digital resources;

– the Beaune municipal archives and library showcase[24] the city of Beaune and its resources;

– in the United States, the University of Florida libraries also have their own YouTube channel.

---

21 https://www.reddit.com/; https://www.quora.com/.
22 http://www.bibliosansfrontieres.org/.
23 https://www.youtube.com/user/genevebm.
24 https://www.youtube.com/channel/UC7gSkHsYnuqvzpu9WzH7OPA/videos.

Another consequence of the emergence of YouTube and the previously mentioned phenomenon of recommendation systems is the increase in the number of book and reading prescribers on the Internet, known as Booktubers: a contraction of the words "book" and "YouTube", a Booktuber is an individual who is filmed commenting on a recent reading and who then broadcasts the video on YouTube. As with any social network, it is possible to subscribe to the chosen channel. The phenomenon seems to be more Anglophone than Francophone.

Reflecting the current online trend, the videos of the most famous English-speaking booktubers (polandbananasBOOKS, jessethereader and katytastic) have been viewed more than 12 million times and each have over 200,000 subscribers... French-speaking Booktubers include Les lectures de Nine and Mathieu M (Enjoy Books)[25].

7.2. Digital archiving of documents

Alongside – or in addition to – service, monitoring and social platforms, other platforms have been set up to make scientific knowledge and information accessible.

They concern the open access archiving of documents, some of them using cloud computing.

> Unlike (or in addition to) traditional computing, which sees data stored on a proprietary server (close to where it is produced), cloud computing is a remote infrastructure: computing power and storage are managed by remote servers to which users connect via a secured Internet link. The storage capacity and computing power are adapted to the needs of the users.
>
> For the general public, cloud computing takes the form of digital data storage and sharing services such as Box, Dropbox, Microsoft OneDrive or

---

25 https://www.youtube.com/user/UFlibraries, https://www.youtube.com/user/poland bananasBOOKS, https://www.youtube.com/user/jessethereader, https://www.youtube.com/user/Katytastic, https://www.youtube.com/user/LesLecturesdeNiNe/videos, https://www.youtube.com/user/lacacahuete83140/videos, https://www.youtube.com/user/lecturedelivres/videos.

> Apple iCloud, where users can store personal content (such as photos, videos, music or documents) and access it anywhere in the world, from any connected terminal.

Box 7.4. *Cloud computing*

7.2.1. *Document archiving: an overview of open access*

In 2003, a number of countries signed up to the Berlin Declaration[26]. This declaration states, in particular:

> In order to realize the vision of a broad and accessible representation of knowledge, the future Web has to be sustainable, interactive and transparent. Content and software tools must be openly accessible and compatible. Establishing open access as a worthwhile procedure ideally requires the active commitment of each and every individual producer of scientific knowledge and holder of cultural heritage. Open access contributions include original scientific research results, raw data and metadata, source materials, digital representations of pictorial and graphical materials and scholarly multimedia material[27].

Open access electronic publications must meet two conditions in order to comply with this statement:

1) Authors and right holders grant a free and irrevocable right of access to these publications for any user. Users may reproduce them, transmit them, display them in public or distribute derived works, provided that the author is credited.

---

26 https://openaccess.mpg.de/68042/BerlinDeclaration_wsis_fr.pdf.

27 Berlin Declaration on Open Access to Knowledge in the Sciences and Humanities, 2003.

2) A complete version of the publication and its appendices is deposited on a long-term basis in at least one online archive, managed by a public body and complying with the technical standards of the Open Archives Initiative (OAI).

The majority of academic and research communities in developed countries, notably in France, adhere to the principle of open archives and make it almost mandatory for members of their community. Some examples of open archives:

– BioMed Central[28] contains an evolving portfolio of some 300 peer-reviewed journals, sharing discoveries from the science, technology, engineering and medical research communities;

– CERN Document Server[29] contains library records and full-text documents for researchers working in particle physics and related fields. It also contains preprints, published articles, books, journals and photographs;

– The National Scientific Research Center (*Centre National de la Recherche Scientifique,* CNRS), through its Center for Direct Scientific Communication (*Centre pour la Communication Scientifique Directe*[30], CCSD), offers researchers open archives in physics, mathematics and neuroscience, as well as in information and communication sciences and human and social sciences;

– The HAL[31] (*Hyper Article en Ligne*) server contains articles and, since June 2001, theses[32]. The main archives that it hosts are:

- HAL-Inria[33] (*Institut National de Recherche en Informatique et en Automatique,* National Information and Automation Technology Research Institute),

---

28 http://www.biomedcentral.com.
29 http://cdsweb.cern.ch.
30 https://www.ccsd.cnrs.fr/.
31 http://www.hal.inserm.fr.
32 http://hal.archives-ouvertes.fr.
33 http://hal.inria.fr.

- HAL-SHS[34] (*Sciences humaines et sociales*, Humanities and Social Sciences),

- Inserm[35] (*Institut National de la Santé et de la Recherche Médicale*, National Health and Medical Research Institute),

- TEL[36] (*Thèses en Ligne*, Theses Online);

– Codata is an international scientific committee established since 1966: it offers databases, holds conferences and publishes books[37];

– the Inist open access site[38].

7.2.2. Dissemination methods

There are two methods by which an author can distribute articles in accordance with the Berlin Declaration:

– Self-archiving: any author can deposit their articles directly onto an open archive platform. These documents must comply with OAI standards[39] to enable search engines to index them.

– Publication in alternative journals: these new journals include articles deposited in open archives, funded by the Open Society Institute (OSI). The PubMed Central database of the National Library of Medicine in the United States hosts multiple scientific and medical journals of this type. In Switzerland, the Western Switzerland University Conference (*Conférence Universitaire Suisse Occidentale*, CUSO) and the Swiss National Science Foundation also adhere to these principles: the universities have open archive systems or institutional servers, as well as open archive guidelines.

---

34 http://halshs.archives-ouvertes.frHAL.
35 http://inserm.fr.
36 http://tel.archives-ouvertes.fr.
37 http://www.codata.org.
38 http://openaccess.inist.fr.
39 Open Archives Initiative.

Numerous initiatives are emerging in France, where, like the Anglo-Saxon countries, the science sector is best represented. As it was seen previously, the CNRS, through its intermediary the CCSD, offers archives in all fields through the HAL platform[40]. A memorandum of understanding between the major scientific institutions and universities designates HAL as the national database for archiving French scientific articles.

In a documentation service (relating to scientific or medical publications from a research laboratory) or a special library, setting up an open archive makes it possible to offer a digital library service accessible to all users. The role of the information professional is both to encourage researchers to publish in open archives and to find articles that are a useful complement to more traditional information research. To do this, it is necessary to verify that the documents are correctly indexed, especially if this has been done by the author. Documentalists and librarians can play a leading role in setting up open archives, which diversifies and enhances both their profession and the range of documents available. By working in complementarity with scientists, they bring their know-how to process this new type of information and stimulate the enrichment of open archives.

Box 7.5. *The mediating role of the information professional in relation to open archives*[41]

There are two possible ways to publish in open access.

– The "green road" consists of authors depositing their publications themselves on open access servers: this is self-archiving or self-publishing, according to the Berlin Declaration.

– The "gold road" consists of entrusting the publication to a commercial publisher on a server open to any user. Funding is provided by a fee from the author or his/her research organization.

---

40 https://hal.archives-ouvertes.fr/.
41 The "mediation" aspect is mainly developed in Part 4.

7.2.3. *European Open Access Policy*

Within its Horizon 2020 program[42], the European Commission aims to generalize open access to research publications and introduce open access to research data in certain cases. Horizon 2020 includes the obligation to ensure open access to publications resulting from the research it will have financed, on pain of financial penalty. What is the scope of the obligation?

– it concerns all peer-reviewed publications related to the results generated by the recipient;

– beneficiaries are also encouraged, where possible, to make all data necessary for the validation of the results presented in the publication or draft publication available in open access. This is not an obligation, unlike the data that is part of Open Research Data pilot projects;

– recipients are also encouraged to make monographs, books, conference proceedings and so on, published informally and not controlled by journals, available in open access.

Open access does not mean an obligation to publish. The decision to publish or not is the author's. It also does not mean that the author no longer has the right to exploit the results from the publication. The result will have been protected before publication.

What is the objective? The aim is to provide free and wide-ranging online access to all reusable scientific information for all users:

– user rights: at the very least, reading, downloading and printing rights;

– potential additional rights: the right to copy, distribute, search, link and index (not exhaustive).

---

42 http://www.horizon2020.gouv.fr/cid82025/le-libre-acces-aux-publications-aux-donnees-recherche.html.

How are authors protected? Authors are entitled to respect for the integrity of their work, so they must be properly acknowledged and cited according to the usual standards.

The European Commission encourages authors to retain their copyright and to use Creative Commons licenses.

8

Other Technologies for Library Transformation

Other technologies appear to be gaining in popularity at the moment and are seeing some application in the information world. These include blockchain, virtual reality, artificial intelligence (AI) and robotics.

8.1. Blockchain[1]

This technology is currently mainly used in the field of cryptocurrencies, in particular Bitcoin, which is an immaterial currency based on a blockchain.

> A blockchain is a distributed database system that makes transaction history unfalsifiable[2].

Blockchain is useful in the context of transactions: each transaction has a digital fingerprint associated with it so that it can be identified. This technology could be applied to interlibrary loans, academic

---

1 Section inspired by: Fourmeux, T. (2019). Est-ce que les bibliothèques ont besoin de la *blockchain* pour être disruptives ? *Biblio Numericus* [Online]. Available at: https://biblionumericus.fr/.

2 Cavazza, F. (2016). Définitions et enjeux [Online]. Available at: https://fredcavazza.net/tag/blockchain/.

publications (peer reviews), open archive repositories, title delivery or to assist in the development of a universal library card. However, it needs to be better conceptualized in libraries so that professionals can apply it effectively, although mastery of the technology may not be necessary for its use/appropriation in the field, as with other technologies. Explanations by specialists are already a first step towards understanding it.

Blockchain would be effective in managing the data generated by library activity: this is Open Data. Currently, library data is stored in secure repositories, held by library suppliers (providers, digital resources and so on). Access to this data is therefore not straightforward and it should be added that governance often results in a lack of transparency. It appears that the benefit of linking it to a blockchain would be improved visibility and traceability.

Another aspect concerns digital books and digital rights management, which could benefit from better protection.

However, this technology is expensive and requires technically skilled personnel to regularly update and maintain the blockchain. It also remains to be seen whether it is compatible with GDPR and the right to be forgotten, since it is precisely designed not to forget anything.

8.2. Augmented/virtual reality in libraries

Augmented reality (AR) is a variation of virtual reality. It allows the enrichment of the real world by using the potential offered by digital information. Often misunderstood, it is still considered science fiction. From its beginnings in the 1960s, this technology has been used in science, industry and military affairs, due to its cost, the complexity of its development and the infrastructure required. With the development of mobile technologies, especially devices and tablets that bring together all the necessary components to make it work, AR can now take a more prominent place in the real world and in everyday life.

Cultural institutions, mainly those in English-speaking countries, were the first to understand the huge potential offered by such a technology, in education, for example, or to bridge the gap between physical and digital services. QR codes and geolocalization are becoming increasingly commonplace and increasingly widely used and they are the primary components of AR. Let us now take a quick look at the history of AR.

8.2.1. *A brief history of augmented reality*

The term "augmented reality" was first introduced in 1992 by Tom Caudell and David Mizell, scientists working for Boeing, to describe computerized reality. Two years later, in 1994, two professors and engineers, Paul Milgram and Fumio Kishino, wrote about a mixed reality: in this model, there was a real side and on the other, a complete virtual one, both of which could be merged into a so-called mixed reality. In 1997, a second definition was provided by researcher Ronald Azuma:

> Augmented reality allows the user to see the real world, with virtual objects superimposed upon or composited with the real world [...] it would appear to the user that the virtual and real objects coexisted in the same space, similar to the effects achieved in the film *Who Framed Roger Rabbit?*[3]

To be considered as such, AR has the following three characteristics:

– combination of the real and the virtual;

– real-time interaction;

– the 3-D alignment of real and virtual environments.

---

3 Azuma, R. (1997). A survey of augmented reality. *Presence: Teleoperators and Virtual Environments*, 6(4), 355–385.

8.2.2. *Augmented reality explained*

AR broadens the individual's perception of the real world by superimposing digital information. It does not replace the real environment as virtual reality does, but complements it.

Different types of technologies can be combined, as they contribute to

> blurring the boundaries between the physical and virtual environment to provide context and location-based information and interaction[4].

Thus, the information added to reality is not necessarily three-dimensional or two-dimensional, but can take the form of a web page that opens on a mobile terminal or an action that is automatically activated (such as sending an SMS or dialing a phone number).

Several technologies are associated with virtual/AR:

– two-dimensional markers or QR codes;

– augmented objects;

– geolocalization;

– near-field communication (NFC).

In libraries, these technologies can be used to facilitate public access to the world of information: QR codes for circulation in the library, AR to bring a book to life for a user or to explain how the service works, RFID (Radio Frequency Identification) chips in documents and so on.

8.3. Artificial intelligence and robotics

There is much debate about the arrival of AI and robotization in the service sector. Some libraries are already using robots to guide their

---

[4] Jordan, B. (2009). Blurring boundaries: The "Real" and the "Virtual" in hybrid spaces. *Human Organization*.

users around their premises (in Germany, Japan and Singapore) or answer some simple questions (such as finding a book or a particular area). Will these make librarians redundant? This would appear a bit premature. What is certain is that the emergence of AI will bring about upheavals in the organization of work, which has already been the case with the computerization of society, the arrival of the Internet and the introduction of social networks, without libraries disappearing.

> The computerization of catalogues, the development of RFID, lending automation, and the presence of robots have freed up working time so that library professionals can concentrate on other activities, such as mediation with users[5].

However, some activities in libraries cannot be performed by robots or computer programs (such as searching for information, which can quickly become complex):

> Deep learning technologies are unique in that they do not follow explicit rules to offer solutions to problems. They integrate knowledge in the same way that a child learns to recognize the objects around him. However, whereas a child only needs three examples to learn to recognize a cat, it will take thousands to train a neural network[6].

The idea of collaboration between human and machine seems to be more realistic at present, as well as the potential for the librarian to be freed from a number of repetitive tasks. In his blog *Biblio Numericus*, already mentioned, Thierry Fourmeux gives the example of the AuRoSS robot in Singapore, designed to automate the tasks of inventory and book storage, which require a significant amount of human input. The robot scans the shelves at night, identifies

---

5 Fourmeux, T. (2019). Les bibliothèques sont-elles menacées par l'automatisation et l'intelligence artificielle ? [Online]. Available at: https://biblionumericus.en/2019/04/06/les-bibliotheques-sont-elles-menacees-par-lautomatisation-and-artificial-intelligence/.
6 Champain, V. and Mabille, B. (2019). Tribune. *Les Échos*.

documents that are not in the right place and generates a report: librarians can then intervene quickly and efficiently. The accuracy rate is 99% and so this is an undeniable time-saver for librarians.

PART 4

Marketing

9

Marketing Dimensions in Libraries

9.1. Digital marketing

One of the dimensions of marketing that is becoming predominant is online or digital marketing, which includes all marketing practices used on digital media and channels. In an environment where digitization is on the increase, digital marketing has become an essential means of communication. Companies, institutions and libraries need to maintain their online reputation and digital identity and establish a permanent interaction with their customers/users/readers if they want a place in the new digital age. Shopping will soon mostly be done online and social and cultural life will be organized through social networks. To not use digital marketing is simply a recipe for failure, both in the short or long term, and will render the institution or service being promoted invisible.

There are several main objectives of digital marketing. The various disciplines of digital marketing are essentially aimed at developing customer relations, the relationship with the user, which is one of the major concerns of libraries and information services. The aim is to increase the awareness of these services, which have not been promoted for a long time. Several techniques can be used:

– increasing website traffic: the important thing is to generate "traffic" (interactions) on the Internet and to create interactions with the public. The site must therefore be updated and offer news and content that the public may or may not like. The referencing of the site by search engines is also essential to ensure that it is visible and then visited;

– building user loyalty to ensure that visitors return to the site and use the services and content offered. For example, this can be achieved through recommendations about works or reviews of a particular activity. The brand image of the institution is important in this loyalty building;

– influencing the target audience: social networks, which allow the creation of online communities, have a strong potential for attraction and extend and amplify the actions of the physical target groups that already exist in the libraries.

Digital marketing includes several aspects that can be very useful for libraries, but we will consider only a few directly related to them. The first aspect that we have already covered is that of data curation[1]; the second is the "mediation" aspect, and more specifically "online mediation", which will be developed at length.

9.2. The user at the heart of transformation

9.2.1. *Addressing ongoing challenges*

The Internet is posing many challenges for libraries. While the use of libraries and information and documentation services as a means of obtaining information is no longer essential, the social Web does lead to regular online contact with users. Users are becoming increasingly central and

– give their opinion (on blogs);

– occasionally exchange between each other when user panels are created (on forum or exchange platforms);

– react to responses provided to them by librarians (via a virtual reference service);

– write book reviews (to be added to the library catalogue);

---

[1] See Part 3.

– provide recommendations through recommender systems that also affect libraries;

– index documents or images with tags;

– evaluate websites, the type of information provided and the response given and so on.

> With social media, libraries are reaching out to their users: there are several options, one of which is crowdsourcing, the practice of obtaining services, ideas or content, by soliciting contributions from a large group of people, especially from an online community, rather than from traditional employees or suppliers.
>
> Some large institutions have been quick to understand how to use such a tool: one of the best known examples is the New York Public Library, which has over 3,000 photos (non-copyrighted) available on its Flickr page. Anyone can "tag" (attach a keyword), comment on and take notes on the images, just like any other Flickr photo. This benefits not only the community but also the collections themselves. Many photos lack details, such as when they were taken, who took them and the names and places photographed. While this information is being collected by Flickr members, the quality of library records can be improved. The Swiss National Library has launched a project for the proofreading and correction of the digitized[2] Swiss press by its users.
>
> The US corporation Dell has been a pioneer in launching crowdsourcing platforms and is constantly involving its users in the development of new products. Its latest platform is Ideastorm.com with the tagline, "Ideastorm turns your ideas into reality". As of May 2013, 18,876 ideas had been submitted and 531 implemented.

Box 9.1. *Crowdsourcing in libraries*

9.2.2. *Capturing the user's attention online*

This change in the relationship between libraries, information services and their users is also due to the change in the behavior of the users themselves on the Internet: one of the major difficulties is

---

2 http://www.e-newspaperarchives.ch.

managing to capture, and then keep, their attention, whether on site or online.

It has been demonstrated that the attention span of a web user is only a few minutes when they are browsing a site[3]. This is due to an attention deficit, which is a syndrome that is becoming increasingly widespread, as reported by numerous studies, and which primarily affects the younger generations[4], characterized by, for example, difficulty concentrating for more than a few minutes on a subject, mood swings, sleep disorders and memory problems. Adults are, of course, not exempt and there are therapeutic treatments that can be used to cure these disorders[5]. The causes are well known: excessive computer workload, mobile phones, screens in general and social networks. It is also difficult to concentrate when the flow of information is continuous, new information arriving every few minutes. What can librarians do to better engage their users? It seems that a marketing approach can help libraries to better understand these behaviors and to better capture their attention by offering new services.

Another challenge has been added in recent years, which further weakens the position of libraries: (apparent) greater control of information and search engines by users is leading to a lower level of reliance on the skills of librarians.

How, in the face of such different challenges (societal or psychological, as well as technological), can we continue to maintain the attention of users on-site or online? There is obviously no magic formula for capturing an audience (or audiences), but it is possible to propose a method, a concrete "action plan", a global marketing approach.

---

3 See the revealing statistics from the Statistics Brain Research Institute: http://www.statisticbrain.com/attention-span-statistics/ and BJ Media: http://www.bjmedia.ca/infographie-le-temps-dattention-des-internautes-capter-lattention-et-pousser-a-laction/.
4 La Recherche (2015). Trouble de l'attention chez l'enfant : reconnaissance officielle. *La Recherche/L'actualité des sciences* [Online]. Available at: https://www.larecherche.fr/sant%C3%A9/trouble-de-lattention-chez-lenfant-reconnaissance-officielle.
5 HUG (2021). Trouble du déficit de l'attention – hyperactivité (TDA-H) chez l'adulte [Online]. Available at: available at: http://www.hug-ge.ch/sites/interhug/files/documents/tdah.pdf.

9.3. Adopting a five-step marketing approach

As a long-term strategic approach, library marketing allows us to stay as close as possible to users' expectations, while demonstrating its value – and therefore its profitability – to management. This section outlines a five-point methodology for conducting such a project.

In the face of numerous hazards (mostly economic, as seen in Part 1) or new uses of information (social and digital), which often undermine or lessen it, the information function is both weakened and energized within organizations. Marketing allows for a rethinking of the service or the library and what it offers, by calling into question the visibility of this function and even extending it.

This technique, which originated on the other side of the Atlantic, was, for a long time, reserved for companies only, before being introduced in the field of information–documentation, but with some reservations:

> Back home, in the cultural community, the word "marketing" is almost a dirty word.[6]

Fifteen years later, the value of marketing is well established, as it enables information services to promote themselves, while at the same time matching supply and demand for documents. Marketing techniques are helping to improve the image of the documentation service and the library, insofar as they match users with needs and products with services. However, how to do this? What kind of actions should be taken to prove to management or users that the service is an indispensable strategic tool? The following are the key points for a successful marketing project within a service:

1) Identification of missions and target audiences: clarifying the essential orientation of the service is the first step in any marketing approach. The direction of the project will depend on this essential analysis: should it be focused on its organization (which will therefore reduce the project scope) or on the user? It is therefore essential to be

---

6 de Lepinay, J.-Y. (2005). *Documentaliste – Sciences de l'information*, 6, 41.

sure of what the management expects from the service: does it want to see it open up to a new audience or to simply know what it is used for in order to decide whether or not it should survive? These are all questions that will help identify the target audience for future marketing operations.

> Setting up projects to show management that you exist has become extremely common. This is not an easy thing to do, as few professionals are trained in library marketing. But it is now essential.[7]

2) Who will lead the project? The next step is to identify who will be implementing the marketing project: is the team involved or is it the manager's responsibility? Will the department carry out these operations itself or is it possible to call on the company's communications department (assuming there is one), whose job it is? Another possibility, if the budget allows, may be to call on an external service provider. It is also not uncommon to see a mixture of these different options and multiple sub-projects should be considered without hesitation as part of a global marketing approach.

3) Surveys: it is strongly recommended that a library marketing project be approached through market research. This involves carrying out surveys of users of the service or of a specific panel of people. The objectives of these surveys are to assess the information needs of users, to find out how they perceive the service and the information products offered and how these may or may not meet their expectations. Detailed analysis should be carried out in order to evaluate the sociological and sociocultural contexts of the user, their behavior with regard to information (such as selection, exploitation and evaluation of information), the psychological context and the personality of users: their motivations and the levels of response provided – cognitive, affective and behavioral – while, of course, remaining within the limits of personal data.

4) New service offers: analysis of the survey results will help to define the precise outline of the marketing project. Indeed, this will

---

[7] Accart, J.-P. (2019). *Archimag*, 325.

make it possible to identify new user needs: should the service offered be improved (opening times, reception, online presence and so on)? Should new information products be created? Do users' expectations require the team to acquire new skills?

All these results must then be compared with what the team is prepared to invest in terms of time and resources, in order to identify the main development strands for the service. They can be submitted to management in the following way: "We have had such-and-such feedback from our users, so we would like to go in such-and-such a direction. What resources can we obtain to achieve this?" Financial support from the top is essential, but not decisive, as it is always possible to make low-cost improvements by never losing sight of the results of the survey. The work is never wasted, as it at least allows for a review of the service at some point. This will, in any case, be a positive outcome for the team.

5) Communication: once new library services and products that are better adapted to the expectations of users have been set up, it will be necessary to communicate about them. Through communication, the service will be more visible, in terms of the benefits that it offers, its role and its place within the organization. The idea is to encourage global communication, by creating the need and the desire to use documentation, by arousing curiosity.

The organization's internal communication materials are essential and totally free tools for promoting new products. They can also serve as a reminder to those who might have doubts about their usefulness or even of their existence. Materials should be multiplied, from internal newsletters to the annual activity report of the organization, including posters, the intranet, the staff welcome booklet or even interventions during meetings.

The documentation service and the library's own communication materials should also be used to the full (e.g. notice boards, employee directories, newsletters, Internet/intranet pages for the service, blogs, organization of exhibitions and thematic displays).

External materials allow the department to present a dynamic image outside the organization and thus to reinforce its image within it. Specialist press should be contacted and participation in networks, associations or professional events (conferences, trade fairs and so on) should be strongly encouraged. The power of social networks can heighten communication, at a lower cost.

9.4. Everyday marketing

Although the implementation of such projects may seem difficult (given, in most cases, the internal conditions of the organization), small actions can sometimes be sufficient to survey the expectations of users and to communicate on the service and this is something that many departments are already doing. Examples include:

– sending a regular e-mail to the different types of users, in order to get feedback from them or to inform them;

– identifying and contacting individual prescribers;

– distributing small flyers around the organization may be enough to remind everyone of the value and worth of the service.

It is a state of mind, an ongoing and regular process that can ensure that the service is not forgotten. This approach consists, first and foremost, of orienting all the actions of the library or service towards the user. It is therefore a "political", strategic action that must be decided upon, written down and disseminated: in this case, it is very useful to rely on the skills of a marketing communications department, but, in the absence of such a department, it will be necessary to use resources within the project team.

This action is based on a "vision" of the library, which is defined and shared by the management of the library (or of the organization in general) and stems either from public cultural activity or from strategic decisions in the private sector.

Elected officials, and political decision-makers in general, are very sensitive to the "user public" aspect of the library (they tend to be very interested in statistics on attendance and use) and to the impact that the library can have in the city or institution and the company. The vision for the future must be discussed with them (they may need to be convinced), and it then takes the form of a policy and mission statement centered on users and the services to be put in place.

One example of a "vision" may be the will to provide online services identical to those offered on site, in order to reach the greatest number of users, in the near future, including: library resources in the form of links to controlled sources and classified according to the system adopted by the library, such as the bookmarks of the Swiss National Library, classified according to the Dewey Classification and identical to the reference works in the rooms open to the public. Users thus have the same system for finding information, whether on site or online[8]. Another example is that of an on-site exhibition where additional interesting information can be found on the library's website, such as reports, links, videos or various interviews. The virtual exhibitions of the *Bibliothèque Nationale de France* are very popular[9].

---

8 http://www.nb.admin.ch/dienstleistungen/swissinfodesk/01860/index.html?lang=fr.
9 http://expositions.bnf.fr/index.php.

10

The User at the Heart: Mediation

Putting the user at the heart means convincing all the staff of the library or information service to be true agents of the change undertaken, from the secretary to the storekeeper, from the curator of old books to the webmaster.

Each must integrate the vision elucidated by management, adhere to it (hence the value of involving staff in the initial reflection) and adapt it to their daily

– telephone responses to users;

– ways in which they welcome the public;

– paying attention to questions asked;

– desire to be proactive in meeting the needs of users, examples being the reception service of the Amsterdam Public Library[1] or the Kornhausbibliothek in Berne[2], Switzerland, who have set up the "walking reference", which is a way of reaching out to users without being too insistent.

This aspect of the marketing approach, involving staff and making them proactive, is really one of the essential points. This requires a great deal of attention and may require training, including awareness

---

1 http://www.oba.nl/.
2 http://www.kornhausbibliotheken.ch/.

of reception and interpersonal skills and training in reference to interviewing, information retrieval and design thinking. The image of the library depends, to a large extent, on the team in place and its behavior towards users.

With the notion of "the user at the heart", it is also important to regularly consult the public (every two or three years) by carrying out a satisfaction survey, as required as part of any marketing approach. Defining target audiences, conducting a satisfaction survey (on site or online), setting up a user panel: all these measures make it possible to develop or consolidate the vision that has been set out. The mediation aspect then takes on its full meaning.

10.1. Keeping in touch with the user: mediation

One of the origins of the development of the concept of mediation – or intermediation – since the 1980s and 1990s is the arrival of information technologies, which make it possible to orientate information services and benefits differently and to propose other, new or complementary services and benefits. The intervention domains of information professionals have expanded considerably:

– training of users in computer tools (e.g. querying online catalogues, databases, search engines and the use of online translation);

– assistance and support (in the use of the service(s) offered);

– development of new information products;

– application of marketing techniques and information monitoring.

Mediation is multifaceted and can be seen from the point of view of the information professional, the user or the library resource itself. It is becoming more widespread with the thematic organization of resources offered by some institutions[3]: a number of information

---

3 BBF (2001). Les Topographies du savoir. *Bulletin des bibliothèques de France*, 1 [Online]. Available at: http://bbf.enssib.fr [Accessed August 20, 2019].

media (such as books, periodicals, audiovisuals and databases), which would previously have been distributed in the traditional way, separately, are grouped together around a thematic hub. Access to information is no longer based on the location of the medium itself (the reference room, the periodicals room, the multimedia area and so on), but on a particular theme. The use of a specialist in the theme, an expert, strengthens the service offering and each subject area may have its own specialist reference desk.

Another type of mediation is the proposal, in various sectors, of personalized research assistance services, with the help of a professional. This service is called *Book a Librarian*, which allows users to book the services of a competent professional. This trend towards individualized services is certainly a way forward for the information professions and also corresponds to current developments in society, with increasingly personalized products and services on offer.

In parallel with traditional functions, the function of mediation towards new information services involves the acquisition of additional skills and knowledge: technicality, expertise, education and communication.

According to J.-C. Brochard, the author of the blog *Bibliothèque = Public*:

> The fact is that libraries are less and less a required gateway to information and they must develop their mediation activities in access to information and elaborate new service offerings if they want to continue to be valuable to their users. Librarians are, by definition, specialists in information management and retrieval. It seems to me that they have every interest in continuing to develop these skills, while always bearing in mind that it is their responsibility to pass on to the public, who are increasingly required to use complex information retrieval tools on their own, useful knowledge adapted to

their needs about the means available to them for finding and managing information[4].

The notion of mediation clearly implies an important human aspect, as well as a strong relational aspect, with a connection between a demand (from the public) and an offering (from the professional); it is therefore a service relationship. Finally, it has a professional aspect: behavior, attitude and response to a need for information.

Mediation concerns:

– all professions involved in information services and library receptions, such as on-site or online reference and information and guidance services;

– those responsible for training the public, such as in information retrieval, in the catalogue or on the Internet;

– those in charge of administration, such as for the reception of school audiences, young people and other audiences.

10.2. Mediation(s)

Mediation is not communication. Neither is it prescription and it cannot be described as a technical device. If we were to give a current definition in the context of libraries and document services, it would be that mediation is the act of creating a link between information devices (collections, catalogues, databases, portals or platforms) and the public. The important thing is to establish a relationship with users, since libraries are not only a set of resources but they also provide a service, listening and an understanding of needs.

Librarians must make the library as pleasant and welcoming a place as possible, but how do we welcome the public? How is the furniture arranged? How are the documents accessed? We must constantly remind people that the library is an open and friendly place, because users can now turn to other offerings outside the library. The

---

4 Brochard, J.-C. (2011). Bibliothèque = Public [Online]. Available at: http://bibliothequepublic.blogspot.com/.

human dimension, which is as omnipresent in a library as it is in a documentation service, is a strong competitive advantage.

The types of mediation detailed below are part of an overall service policy and are not isolated from the rest. All library staff must be involved in this process, so that they become imbued with this service policy. This implies an upstream reflection with guidelines. Mediation is the emanation of what the library wants to be.

Mediation is therefore, first and foremost, a connection between the public and the library resources and takes the form of a transfer of information: learnings, orientation, assistance, search for information and documents, training in information and so on. This is the most "obvious" type of information mediation or documentary mediation.

10.2.1. *Library mediation*

Often considered as the core business of the librarian, the document (whether paper or digital) must be valued by users. A relationship is created between the document and the user, but mediation does not happen by itself. It is carried out around a service project: the needs of the public must be taken into account, they must be involved in the project and, if possible, they must be included in working groups, user panels must be set up and surveys carried out. How often? Every two or three years, so as not to exhaust users and to obtain a satisfactory response rate. There is a risk an annual gap between surveys is too short and will come round too quickly, ultimately generating few responses.

It is also possible to innovate. A current trend in library mediation is to offer escape games in libraries, such as at the library of the *Ecole Hôtelière de Lausanne* in Switzerland, where an escape game focusing on documentary resources and based on solving enigmas has been established. Students are invited, of course, as well as the teachers and staff of the school. They must follow a library trail and answer questions about the Lausanne Hotel School, which celebrated its

125th anniversary in 2018[5]. The game consists of finding the right information resources to answer the riddles, such as knowing how to use the Dewey Classification to carry out research and search in the right databases. A librarian is present to assist the players. This type of mediation is quite innovative and is a fun way of highlighting documentary resources and access to documents. The Sciences Po library in Paris has also launched an escape game. This is a form of mediation that must, however, be limited in time: the game is limited to 30 minutes so as not to take up too much time for the users.

In fact, it could easily be said that everything is mediation: the way the library is organized to facilitate its use (architecture, colors and furniture chosen, circulation spaces, presentations of information and documents), or how the librarians present themselves and behave, are important elements for successful mediation.

10.2.2. *Social mediation*

Libraries are part of a social environment and a territory. They maintain relationships with other organizations and local associations. In particular, public libraries offer free resources to users, without asking for anything in return. In Germany, the example of libraries and migrants is particularly interesting. Libraries were one of the first sectors to respond with a series of social mediation actions to integrate migrants into German society. For example, they have helped them to compile integration dossiers and assisted them with certain administrative procedures. Language courses have also been offered. Of course, this type of initiative is carried out in perfect agreement with the authorities. Librarians can also contact associations to set up similar programs for the public.

Social mediation is aimed at different audiences, such as immigrants or people from disadvantaged backgrounds, who do not have access to books or culture. It is also aimed at so-called

---

5 https://info.ehl.edu/en/125.

"prevented" audiences, which include prisoners, hospital patients and the disabled. In all these cases, thanks to in-depth work with local associations, archive, library or documentation services can provide answers by setting up adapted resources, services and activities. Remember that a library is a social space that welcomes all types of people. According to Claude Poissenot, a French library sociologist[6], it creates social links and social cohesion. Social mediation is carried out in person.

10.2.3. Cultural mediation

Meetings with authors, exhibitions, concerts, plays, games, festive activities, story times for children: for a long time now, libraries have been organizing events able to attract a varied public, with some success. This is one way of making libraries more visible and more concrete in the eyes of the public, by making use of their (sometimes unknown) collections or local resources (such as history, geography and local culture). Cultural mediation is written into the cultural policies of the city, region, university or country. Cultural mediator positions are created, and recruitment exists for this type of mission. On closer inspection, these positions are rarely full-time. Cultural mediators work part time and rarely all the time, except perhaps in very large establishments of the largest communities, and sometimes suffer from a lack of resources to organize events.

Being a cultural mediator is also one of the most interesting orientations of a librarian's job. Cultural mediation is practiced both in person and virtually.

10.2.4. Digital mediation

The relationship that develops with the user in a real situation can also be developed virtually: digital mediation takes into account the

---

[6] Poissenot, C., Octobre, S., Brisset, I., Peyrelong, M.-F., Jackson, K., Le Bars, S., Boucher, T., Martin, F. (2009). Quelle relation demain ? *Documentaliste-Sciences de l'Information*, 3(46), 58–69.

virtual dimension of networks and facilitates access to digital information. Digital/online mediation takes many forms:

– helping a user who has no access to a computer to bridge the digital divide;

– setting up a question and answer service, such as Le Guichet du Savoir (the Lyon municipal library) or Eurêkoi (the Pompidou Centre public information library);

– creating common interest and sharing communities and accounts on Facebook, Twitter or Instagram.

Presence on social networks must correspond to the policy of the institution. It is about creating a digital identity that reflects the library and its missions. The style must be less institutional than the official website of the institution.

A Facebook page or a tweet offers the opportunity to include humor, but, at the same time, being mindful of posting rules. Before launching themselves on a social network, librarians can get up to speed by following a dedicated training course. Digital mediation is practiced virtually and leads to the social Web, which has developed since its emergence. Frédéric Cavazza, a specialist in social media, defines social media as follows:

> Social media refers to a set of services that allow for the development of conversations and social interactions on the internet or in mobile situations.[7]

The service relationship that develops with the user in a real situation can also be developed virtually.

10.2.5. *Scientific mediation*

Scientific mediation, in the context of digital humanities[8], consists of:

---

7 Cavazza, F. (2009). Une définition des médias sociaux [Online]. Available at: https://fredcavazza.net/2009/06/29/une-definition-des-medias-sociaux/.

– identifying Open Data experiments and practices on the internet, linked to online publications in the humanities and social sciences;

– conducting a literature review;

– writing reports;

– communicating and interacting with researchers.

Scientific mediation is also practiced on YouTube with channels in the human and social sciences that reach out to their audience, or via podcasts of courses and conferences on university and specialist school networks. The Twitter network and the Periscope platform are also viewed by scientists as mediation tools. Scientific mediation is practiced virtually.

Finally, there are two other types of mediation:

– Technological: in the humanities and social sciences, as well as in the sciences, this is practiced through close collaboration between documentalists and researchers. Technological mediation has existed for a long time and has strengthened the role of the documentalist or specialist librarian within scientific institutions and research or pharmaceutical laboratories. It is very specific work, which generally requires degrees in two sciences: biology and pharmacy.

– Pedagogical: this form of mediation is carried out in an educational setting, within school libraries, with teacher-documentalists at documentation and information centers (*Centres de Documentation et d'Information*, CDI, in France) or at universities, in university libraries. Professionals then teach information learning and expertise, known as "information literacy": at a university, this may take the form of a compulsory course with ECTS (European Credit Transfer system) credits, which is the case at the Faculty of Sciences of the University of Geneva.

---

8 The term digital humanities describes a transdisciplinary field, involving methods, devices and heuristic perspectives linked to digital in the field of humanities and social sciences. See: https://tcp.hypotheses.org/318.

Mediation can be one of the components of a successful marketing approach. With digital mediation becoming increasingly important in libraries in recent years, it is not without merit, following on from the presentation of social platforms in Part 3, to point to the visibility of the library through social media, on the one hand (implementing its digital identity), and its personalization through a brand strategy, on the other.

11

The Library's Digital Identity

As an extension of the notion of digital marketing explained at the beginning of Part 4, we must now consider all the dimensions of the library's digital identity. This relatively recent notion of digital identity has become essential, as it is now impossible for institutions and individuals alike not to be present and active on networks and on the Internet. To this end, and as a complement to this chapter, Chapter 10, which deals with social networks from a more technical perspective, should be read. However, it is necessary to see what individual identity comprises before considering the identity of an institution or an organization.

11.1. Defining identity

Starting with the individual, identity (from the Latin *identitas*: the fact of being the same) is the characteristic of that which remains identical to itself[1]. An individual is characterized by their identity; it is their own and is made up of what distinguishes them from others and makes them unique. However, an individual has several identities, which can manifest themselves in different universes, sometimes complementary or distinct or separate: family, friends, school, university, work, participation sports, hobbies, the associative world,

---

1 *Le Robert* Dictionary, 2018.

various social circles and so on. Identity is not one but many. We can therefore refer to "identities", rather than simply "identity".

Legally, a person's identity is recorded in civil status: this is a combination of the date and place of birth, surname, first name and filiation of a person who is legally recognized. Civil status makes it possible to identify a person in a unique way. We distinguish between:

– Social identity: an individual shares a certain number of statuses with the other members of the groups to which they belong (such as gender, age or profession). According to anthropologist Nicole Sindzingre, social identity is inseparable from individuation:

> To identify one or more individuals with others, they must be distinguished from anything they are not[2].

– Cultural identity is the more or less complete adherence of an individual to the norms and values of a culture.

These two identities, social and cultural, are closely linked: an individual, as a social being, cannot construct their identity without taking into account the social and cultural universe in which they are evolving. Identity is therefore not a fixed or finished product, but a constantly evolving process.

According to Philippe Buschini, whether personal, social or cultural, identity is marked by three fundamental attributes:

– "it is that which makes one similar to oneself and different from others";

– "it is made up of values that link the individual to the world";

– "it is evolutionary, the personality of an individual evolving over time"[3].

---

2 Quoted by Dominique Wolton at: http://www.wolton.cnrs.fr/spip.php?article68.
3 Buschini, P. (2009). Identité traditionnelle versus identité numérique.

Before discussing the digital sphere in more detail, it is worth mentioning at the outset that the private sphere is strongly influenced by digital technology in general; the Internet – and social networks in particular – have entered our homes in a big way. All socioprofessional categories are impacted, as well as all age groups, even if the digital divide has not been completely eradicated (age, geography and finances play an important role in this divide). Society, as a whole, and a majority of individuals use information technologies to inform and entertain, to organize vacations, to document themselves, to read, to archive personal documents, to carry out research and so on. The boundary between the private and the digital sphere, a boundary that may have corresponded to the delimitation between private life and working life in the days when computing was primarily a professional activity, no longer exists for some Internet users, and the numbers are increasing.

11.2. From the individual to the group and the library institution

Digital technology, which is transversal, invests in all areas that concern the individual, whether private, civic or professional, with the help of increasingly integrative media, such as mobile phones and tablets.

Access to information has changed irreversibly and has never been easier. Each person's identity, which was private at the outset, is now irrevocably shifting towards the digital world and therefore towards a public domain, open to everyone. There is no longer any separation between private and public life, and also sometimes between private and professional life. This is seen particularly, but not exclusively, when using social networks. Each of us now has a digital identity on the Internet, an identity that Louise Merzeau rightly describes as a digital presence. Highly comparable to the traditional identity in its multidimensional aspect, the digital identity, due to its immaterial nature, is characterized by two distinct but complementary types of information that define the digital individual:

– fragmented information, which is both incontestable and unique: a person's physical coordinates, an IP address, digital certificates, bank accounts, a telephone number and others, assigned by a third-party authority (such as a civil authority, Internet access provider, telecommunications operator or bank);

– so-called multiple information, such as pseudonyms, avatars, comments, blogs, photos and resumes, which are created by individuals themselves.

The sociologist Dominique Cardon proposes a typology of the different forms of online presence and what this implies for individuals.

Five ways of being visible have emerged and are organized according to the combination of digital identity and type of visibility sought:

– "screening or hiding in order to be seen: a profile or an information sheet can display all or part of an identity";

– "chiaroscuro, or being seen to be hiding: participants make visible all or part of their intimate details and their daily life to a social network of close friends, this being not accessible to others";

– "the lighthouse, or show and tell: identity, interests and skills are easily accessible to all. Visibility is based on reputation, numbers of friends, audience and so on";

– "the *lanterna magica*, or being seeing but hidden: these are the avatars created to assume another identity in the virtual world";

– "the post-it, or 'I'm here, I'm doing this': in the form of a platform, participants make their availability and presence visible to all, but only interact with a limited circle of contacts[4]".

While we are witnessing a close interweaving and interdependence between the private and digital spheres, the latter creates the opportunity for multiple identities and digital presences on the Web

---

4 Cardon, D. (2008). Le Design de la visibilité : un essai de typologie du Web 2.0. *Réseaux*, 6(152), 93–137.

and for establishing or re-establishing distinctions between the professional aspect with an adequate profile (a complete and accurate resume on the LinkedIn site can be useful), the social aspect (by subscribing to sites such as Facebook or Twitter), the playful aspect (by creating an avatar) or the institutional presence that can be applied to all social media as digital traces.

11.3. Profiles, behavior and traces on the Internet

Each individual and institution therefore has a digital identity, a certain identifiable personality on the Internet. Although the criteria for private identity, defined above, can be easily attributed to the digital individual, the statuses of the individual and the institution are different, especially on social networks: a major difference is that the digital individual creates their own identity (thanks to a pseudonym or an avatar), they can make it evolve or disappear and can modify it. However, activity on the Internet leaves a certain number of traces that together form a set of identifiable digital traces, detectable by search engines or algorithms.

Olivier Ertzscheid also points out that this digital identity is:

> The reflection of this set of traces, as it appears after "remixing" by search engines.[5]

Digital identity is therefore partly constructed by the individual, more or less consciously, but it is also exposed and staged, particularly by search engines and their lists of results. We have gone from the identifier (assigned by an administration, for example, without any control from interested parties) to the identification (the login/password pair), that allows a user to be authenticated on a service or computer system, and then to this global identity, a double on the networks.

---

5 Ertzscheid, O. (2010). E-réputation, identités numériques : enjeux, outils, méthodologies. Paper, Urfist de Rennes, Rennes.

Digital identity is most often defined as:

> The set of "traces" or "footprints" left by individuals in "digital universes" and, more specifically, as data related to the participation of individuals in socionumerical networks.[6]

Digital identity is a self-construction and is entirely free. A single individual or institution can multiply their number of profiles according to the communities they frequent, thus presenting different facets of a prism: it is not uncommon for a library's digital identity to be present on several social networks at once. These profiles may not be linked to each other, nor to the real person or institution concerned.

The digital identity of an institution or a library is a way of asserting its own personality, or even of its personalization. It would not be complete without the creation of a library brand that characterizes it.

What to remember about social networks?

Why do I go online: business, socializing, gaming, community of interest, shopping? Each goal has its own strategy.

Questioning what I can show and/or say?

My digital identity is not only made up of my first and last name, or pseudonym, but it is also defined by what I show, say or do (especially the sites I visit).

It is best to split the digital identity into four distinct entities: professional, friends, family and personal.

Be aware that anything published can be used without my knowledge, or even against me.

Any requests for services, and especially payments via the Internet, can be added to a commercial database on my tastes and purchases.

---

6 Compiègne, I. (2010). *Les Mots de la société numérique.* Belin, Paris.

It is very difficult to erase cumbersome traces of my time on the Internet. The privacy policy of a social networking site can quickly change.

It is important to know the specificity of each site on which I am active, such as blogs, forums or social networks such as Facebook.

Employers are increasingly turning to the Internet to search for traces left by job applicants.

Box 11.1. *Nine points to remember about social networks, according to François Filliettaz*[7]

---

[7] Filliettaz, F. (2011). Comprendre l'identité numérique. Document, Direction des services d'information, State of Geneva.

12

Adopting a Library Branding Strategy

Library and brand? An unlikely or possible association? Some would say that they are an unlikely couple, but, for some years now, the cultural sector has understood that it cannot do without considering marketing, generally, and the notion of brand, in particular: it merits discussion. Museums and libraries, previously unwilling or inclined to consider their worlds as competitive, are now changing their image and asserting themselves in the public space.

The pioneers of this are primarily the large institutions, often because they are better known and have established reputations. We think of the BnF (Bibliothèque nationale de France) or the Bpi (Bibliothèque publique d'information), their acronyms sometimes being preferred to their full names.

The question of brand has become essential for all types of institutions (private, public, associative), in order to be known and recognized; however, the brand must be based on a system of values, intentions, and promises towards the outside world.

Arguments can be put forward advocating tackling this topic, which originates from marketing and therefore from business and which is perfectly in keeping with today's libraries.

12.1. Defining the brand concept

A trademark is a name, term, sign, symbol, design or any combination thereof used to identify a seller's goods or services and to differentiate them from the competition[1].

For Michel Lepeu, the brand concept relies on five pillars: it must be living, multicultural and multigenerational, ethical and societal[2].

In semiology, the brand is a combination of signs that give a specific meaning to the product. Signs can include the "discourse" around the brand (words, images, communication and so on) and what contributes to its creation (such as advertising agencies, designers and consumers).

The brand concept has taken on an important dimension in recent years. It is a reference point in a consumerist world and a commercial society, but some consumers are increasingly suspicious of brands. Accused of invading the public space, having no ethics and thinking only of profit, brands are, for some, considered as flag bearers of capitalism.

However, brand fetishism is still widespread all over the world. One of the latest strong trends is the marketing of the art market (known as "arteking"), which therefore has an impact on culture generally. This translates into greater visibility of patronage, products and stores designed by artists and exhibitions glorifying brands. Logos live on and brands adapt to the protest and take over the protest discourse. Marketing is becoming aggressive with young audiences. In terms of media, there is confusion at the moment, but some media – online – are breaking away and creating strong or at least recognized brands. While the brands persist, however, cultural resistance is

---

[1] American Marketing Association: https://www.ama.org/.

[2] Accart, J.-P. (2018). Personnaliser la bibliothèque : construire une stratégie de marque et augmenter sa réputation. Paper, Enssib, Villeurbanne.

manifesting itself in various ways, such as the Occupy movement, environmental protests and anti-austerity mobilization[3].

The risks of all-out marketing are very present for cultural institutions and therefore for libraries.

12.2. Brands and libraries

The acceptance of the brand concept by the cultural sphere has met with much reticence and resistance: librarians prefer to talk about communication and mediation with the public, rather than marketing... Can the brand concept be applied to the world of culture, libraries and information services?

This raises other questions: does the library brand have a meaning? Can information professionals and librarians find their way around this concept and integrate it into their daily lives? In the cultural world, the answer is Yes, as in the case of museums. Some libraries have acquired a reputation and are known worldwide by name. Does this mean that every library or information service should develop its own brand? Can the brand be applied to a single service or to a small library? The answer is already provided in the form of some online public services, such as the Bpi's Eurêkoi service[4]. This is a service brand, with its own name, logo, color and slogan – in short, all the attributes of a brand.

While libraries and information services are not directly related to business or commerce – although they have entered the service economy – they do face similar challenges:

---

3 Section inspired by the following article: Zarachowicz, W. (2018). Que reste-t-il de *No Logo* de Naomi Klein, 15 ans après ? *Télérama* [Online]. Available at: https://www.telerama.fr/idees/que-reste-t-il-de-no-logo-de-naomi-klein-15-ans-apres,124097.php.
4 http://www.bpi.fr/en/sites/SiteInstitutionnel/home/la-bibliotheque/offres-culturelles-et-mediations/offres-a-distance/eurekoi.html.

– it is necessary for them to differentiate themselves or risk not surviving in a public space saturated by marketing and advertising;

– there is real competition with other services (private and public);

– it is imperative to create a unique customer experience[5]:

> Customer experience describes the full range of emotions and feelings felt by a customer before, during and after the purchase of a product or service. It is the result of all the interactions a customer may have with the brand or company[6].

A user who frequents information services and libraries accumulates several experiences:

– the place and the use they can make of it;

– the welcome they receive;

– their relationship with information professionals;

– the advice and information they obtain based on their expressed needs;

– the satisfaction of finding information which they either need, or which they had not originally considered. The concept of serendipity applies here: it is about discovering books or documents on shelves or on display tables that they were not initially looking for.

Customer experience can also be measured in terms of the services offered online: the ease of searching a library catalogue; the way information is arranged on a site; the contact opportunities. These all influence customer satisfaction and ultimately enhance the reputation of the library.

---

5 See also Chapter 8, which addresses the issue of user experience from another angle.
6 http://www.definitions-marketing.com/definition/experience-client/.

Can one library differentiate itself from another? How can it be personalized? Building a brand strategy means thinking about the communication and marketing policy to be implemented, giving the library or service an identity (especially if the service is online). This includes the logo, the institutional signature and the value system of the organization. The identity of a library is not easy to establish or define and its image may also – and often does – become blurred or dissolved into that of the stronger or better defined institution to which it belongs.

For small and medium-sized libraries, the most difficult thing is often to give them a unique place when, on an institutional website, all the cultural entities of a city (museum, theater, cultural center) are grouped together. This can be seen as an advantage, as the public has a single point of access to the cultural activities offered. Compared with the large libraries or museums previously mentioned, it would be interesting to see if and how this branding issue can be developed in small and medium-sized libraries.

12.3. The brand world

Creating a brand for a service, institution or organization means positioning them in their own universe; for libraries, this universe may be culture, in general, or books and public reading, in particular, but it may also be the university, if it is a university library, or the field (economics, law, medicine and so on) to which it is attached.

The brand reflects the identity of a place, and it is then possible to emphasize the specificity of the identity of public institutions, such as public service or free access, for example.

The brand thus created reflects a universe and declines it under various conditions. Over time and under various influences, the brand and its concept must evolve and adapt. For a long time, libraries were represented by having books or printed documents on their logos, then later by audiovisual media, to mark the transition to multimedia (in the case of media libraries). They have also been identified by the places where they are established or by the name of a local or national personality (a politician, writer or a president of the Republic). It is important to measure the impact of these different choices: the final choice must be an asset and must even become, if possible, a brand.

These names have often become outdated over time and no longer have the meaning for which they were chosen, such as if the name is linked to an event or a long-forgotten politician. Current names call upon concepts or notions: the example of Lilliad at the University of Lille is revealing. Beneath this name is hidden the fusion of a university library and a learning center in a well-defined place, a building built in 1965 by the architect Noël Le Maresquier, with, unusually, almost no load-bearing walls and being totally glazed over its whole height and its two floors, across 360 degrees. Decorative cloisters surrounded the exterior facade and the building was topped with a glass dome. The building has since been renovated to its original state, and a new library has been added[7].

Libraries – like museums and other cultural venues – are increasingly positioning themselves as open places that can be visited without any particular constraints, without having to justify anything, usually free of charge. This does not mean that they are totally neutral places, since their layout and their organization of space and what is presented there means that they can justify their own existence or, at the very least, be seen as a trusted place.

Today, many libraries are making significant efforts in this direction and implementing what has been described in the previous chapters. However, is it necessary to have to go so far to please and attract the public? The question is worth asking. Do libraries not risk losing their soul by offering something other than what they were designed for? It is not that they should not evolve, but there is also a great risk that libraries may end up losing the public that had already

---

7 https://fr.wikipedia.org/wiki/Lilliad_Learning_Center_Innovation.

been won over. In fact, a recent trade magazine raised just this issue, when referring to the student public under the title: "What if students just want traditional libraries?"[8] According to the studies cited in three American university libraries, students much prefer paper to electronic resources, as well as the traditional services offered by libraries.

---

8 Jost, C. (2019). *Archimag*, 328 [Online]. Available at: https://www.archimag.com/library-edition/2019/10/08/university-students-traditional-libraries.

Conclusion

This book is, without any pretension, intended to be a synthesis of the advances in the world of libraries and information – societal, technical and technological advances, in management, human resources and marketing – that affect the business world and public institutions or associations. The main goal is not to be exhaustive but rather to outline a range of possibilities for the evolution of the library environment.

These possibilities have been described, summarized and analyzed according to their feasibility and practicability, and the main idea of this book is to provide practical and concrete solutions, even if they refer to abstract concepts, such as, for example, new human resources management theories. The practical and practicable side is always in evidence. Divided into four distinct parts, it must be taken into consideration that they are inseparable from each other: project management requires technical knowledge, human resources and marketing techniques.

Most of the experiences cited reflect my own experiences in the field, including case studies. They are therefore real-life experiences that can, of course, be repeated. They are also options for working and living together in a company to improve well-being, especially in relation to teamwork. I must point out here that, without the teams I have met over the course of my career, I would never have been able to undertake such projects, so I thank them sincerely. The case studies cited are not strictly speaking recipes but, rather, recommendations that have proven their worth: how to manage a project, how to apply work rules in a group and how to implement a service platform. The main objective was, therefore, to apply the principle of collaboration and team participation in a transversal mode.

It is important – indeed, imperative – that libraries transform themselves to adapt to today's world: this is a real effort on their part, and, of course, on the part of library staff. There are many external influences, and we must not ignore them. However, this transformation movement is no longer new: after centuries of functioning with traditional rules, since the end of the 19th century, libraries have been radically transforming themselves, while retaining the basic principles that guarantee an efficient management of resources and knowledge, principles that have been applied on a large scale. Technology is playing an increasingly important role, as are new management rules and other ways of managing staff. The theme of marketing is also relevant to libraries.

These aspects have been presented and developed throughout this book, while considering a certain philosophy relating to libraries: the importance of the user at the heart of their reflections; the consideration of user needs; the development of services and related benefits; knowledge commons; the library place as an open, free and unrestricted place; the competences and aptitudes of its staff.

References

Part 1 – The Environment and Society

Confland, D. (1997). *Économie de l'information spécialisée. Valeur, usages professionnels, marchés*. ADBS, Paris.

David, P.A. (2002). Une introduction à l'économie et à la société du savoir. *Revue internationale des sciences sociales*, 171, 13–28.

Drucker, P. (1989). *Les Nouvelles réalités. De l'État-providence à la société du savoir*. InterEditions, Paris.

Goldfinger, C. (1994). *L'Utile et le futile. L'Économie de l'immatériel*. Odile Jacob, Paris.

Jaouan, C. and Jeanroy-Chasseux, C. (2019). *Espaces de création numérique en bibliothèque*. Association des bibliothécaires de France, Paris.

Lankes, R.D. (2018). Exigeons de meilleures bibliothèques : plaidoyer pour une bibliothéconomie nouvelle [Online]. Available at: http://ateliers.sens-public.org/exigeons-de-meilleures-bibliotheques/index.html [Accessed November 10, 2019].

Lessing, L. (2005). *L'Avenir des idées. Le sort des biens communs à l'heure des réseaux numériques*. Presses universitaires de Lyon, Lyon.

Machlup, F. (1984). *Knowledge: Its Creation, Distribution and Economic Significance. Vol. III. The Economics of Information and Human Capital*. Princeton University Press, Princeton.

Mayère, A. (1997). *La Société informationnelle*. L'Harmattan, Paris.

Petit, P. (1998). *L'Économie de l'information. Les Enseignements des théories économiques.* La Découverte, Paris.

Reich, R. (1993). *L'Économie mondialisée.* Dunod, Paris.

Part 2 – Human Resources and Management

Archimag (2007). *Manager et développer son service info-doc. Guide pratique.* Archimag, Paris.

Aubry, C. (2015). *Scrum : le guide pratique de la méthode agile la plus populaire.* Dunod, Paris.

Besner, J. (2002). Une bibliothèque performante où il fait bon travailler : leadership, coaching et gestion des ressources humaines. *Argus*, 31(3), 17–20.

Bouthillier, F. (2002). La sélection du personnel : petit guide à l'usage des gestionnaires de bibliothèques et de services d'information. *Argus*, 31(3), 12–16.

Chevalier, B. (2000). *Le Documentaliste, manager de son équipe.* ADBS, Paris.

Collignon, A. and Schöpfel, J. (2016). Méthodologie de gestion agile d'un projet. Scrum – les principes de base. *I2D – Information, données & documents*, 53, 12–15.

Debrion, P. (2000). La gestion des ressources humaines. *Bulletin des bibliothèques de France*, 1, 71–74.

Illiano, M.-O. and Scalla, A. (2018). Les méthodes agiles en bibliothèque. *Mémoire d'étude*, Université de Lyon et Enssib, Lyon.

Koenig, M.-H. (2018). *Accompagner les transformations du travail en bibliothèque.* Éditions du Cercle de la Librairie, Paris.

Le Boterf, G. (1994). *De la compétence : essai sur un attracteur étrange.* Éditions d'Organisation, Paris.

Letondal, A.-M. (2007). *L'Encadrement de proximité. Quels rôles dans les changements d'organisation ?* ANACT, Paris.

Lettelier, L. (2013). *Management participatif, la coopération au service de la performance.* Ellipses, Paris.

Minzberg, H. (2007). *Le Manager au quotidien*. Éditions d'Organisation, Paris.

de Miribel, M. (2016). *Diriger une bibliothèque. Un nouveau leadership.* Éditions du Cercle de la Librairie, Paris.

Perales, C. (2015). *Conduire le changement en bibliothèque. Vers des organisations apprenantes.* Presses de l'Enssib, Villeurbanne.

Stoddart, L. (2012). Emerging leadership opportunities and new roles for knowledge professionals. *Business Information Review*, 29(4), 215–222.

Part 3 – Library Tools and Technology

Accart, J.-P. (2016). *La Médiation à l'heure du numérique*. Éditions du Cercle de la Librairie, Paris.

Accart, J.-P. and Rivier, A. (2010). *Mémento de l'information numérique*. Éditions du Cercle de la Librairie, Paris.

Beudon, N. (2017). Le vocabulaire du design thinking. *I2D – Information, données & documents*, 54(1), 32–33.

Dupin, C. (2014). *Guide pratique de la veille*. Éditions Klog, Rouen.

Etches, A. and Schmidt, A. (2017). Utile, utilisable, désirable. *Bulletin des bibliothèques de France*, 11, 189–191.

Le Ven, E. (2016). Innovation : penser "expérience utilisateur" peut faire la différence. Archimag [Online]. Available at: https://www.archimag.com/vie-numerique/2016/06/20/innovation-penser-experience-utilisateur-faire-difference.

Papy, F. (2016). *Digital Libraries: Interoperability and Uses.* ISTE Press, London, and Elsevier, Oxford.

Schwaber, K. and Beedle, M. (2002). *Agile Software Development with Scrum.* Pearson Education International, Upper Saddle River.

Vaissaire-Agard, C. (2019). *Concevoir des produits documentaires et des livrables de veille avec le design thinking.* Éditions Klog, Rouen.

Part 4 – Marketing

Accart, J.-P. (2012). La médiation : un peu d'humain dans un monde de technologie. *Argus*, 40(3), 16–18.

Accart, J.-P. (2015). *La Médiation à l'heure du numérique*. Éditions du Cercle de la Librairie, Paris.

Accart, J.-P. (2018). *Personnaliser la bibliothèque : construire une stratégie de marque et augmenter sa réputation*. Presses de l'Enssib, Villeurbanne.

Archimag (2011). *Bibliothèques : les nouveaux usages. Guide pratique*. Archimag.

Calenge, B. (2015). *Les bibliothèques et la médiation des connaissances*. Éditions du Cercle de la Librairie, Paris.

Deschamps, J. (2019). *Mediation: A Concept for Information and Communication Sciences*. ISTE Ltd, London and John Wiley & Sons, New York.

Dujol, L. and Mercier, S. (2017). *Médiations numériques des savoirs – des enjeux aux dispositifs*. Asted, Montreal.

Ibn Khayat, N. (2005). *Marketing des services documentaires*. Asted, Montreal.

de Miribel, M. (2009). *Accueillir les publics : comprendre et agir*. Éditions du Cercle de la Librairie, Paris.

Index

A, B

ABF (*Association des Bibliothécaires de France* – Association of French librarians), 8
access
  open, 96, 100
  to digital information, 128
  to information, 10, 12, 15, 123, 133
ADBS (*Association des Professionnels de l'Information et de la Documentation* – French association of information and documentation professionals), 8
added value, 12, 15, 34
agents of change, 121
algorithm(s), 18, 71, 83, 135
Alma, 83, 84
alternative journals, 98
alumni, 16
AMI Software, 89
animations, 32
approach
  marketing, 92, 130
  quality, 33
Arisem, 89
asset
  cultural, 12
  economic, 12, 15, 34
  public, 15
associations, 7
attention, 53, 113, 114, 121
audience
  "prevented", 127
  target, 112, 116
author(s), 17, 71, 96, 98, 101
auto-archivage, 98
avatars, 88, 134
Berlin Declaration, 96
Big Data, 25, 30, 83
blockchain, 103, 104
Book a Librarian, 123
book reviews, 112
brainstorming, 67, 68
brand, 72, 92, 140
  service, 29
budget, 7, 15, 17, 52, 74, 116
business schools, 16

C

Canada, 16
case study, 56, 63
change management, 47, 53–55
chat, 87
China, 24
civil status, 132
client/customer, 79, 142
close supervision, 65
cloud, 28, 80–84, 95
CNIL (*Commission nationale de l'informatique et des libertés*), 41
communication, 14, 20, 29, 41, 48, 49, 51, 65, 66, 73, 81, 82, 92, 93, 97, 111, 117, 118, 123, 124, 140, 141, 143
  method, 111
communities
  common interest, 128
  online, 87, 112, 113
  virtual communities of users, 72
companies, 6, 9, 13, 18, 24, 50
competition, 140
competitive advantage, 125
consortium, 11
consultants, 9
conversation, 53, 70
Copernic, 89
coproduction, 80
copyright, 12, 21, 101
cost, 21, 82
  of information, 15
coworking, 24, 27
creation
  digital, 25
  process, 69
Creative Commons, 101
crowdsourcing, 113

cultural
  institutions, 105
  mediator(s), 127
curation, 80, 83, 88–91, 112
customer relations, 111
cycle of information, 14

D

data, 40
  hosting, 41
  open, 20
  personal, 39, 40, 42, 116
  research, 100
  security, 42
databases, 10, 87
  professional, 18
decision-making (*see also* political decision-makers), 15, 18
deficit, 114
  attention, 114
  information, 7
delegation, 48, 76
demand, 124
design, 4, 14, 24, 25, 38, 61, 67–69, 84, 85, 87, 92, 122, 140
  thinking, 66
diffusion, 98
Digimind, 89
digital
  content, 86
  divide, 10, 128, 133
  fingerprint, 103
  humanities, 128
  resouces hub, 86
  rights, 104
  technology, 10, 21, 24, 26, 73, 132, 136, 137
digitization, 111
disadvantaged backgrounds, 126

discovery tool, 87
distribution, 73
   of information, 17, 91
document archiving, 96
documentalist(s), 15, 18, 99, 129
documentary
   activities, 9
   pathway, 125
double formation, 129

E, F

EAHIL (European Association for Health Information and Libraries), 8
EBSCO Integrated Library System, 83, 84
economic crisis, 13, 36
economy
   /economics, 5, 13
   information, 14
   of information, 10
   service, 70
education
   lifelong, 31
emotions, 52
empathy, 69
entreprises, 39
escape game(s), 32, 125
ethics/ethical, 50
Europe, 24, 36
European data protection regulations (GDPR), 39
experimentation, 69, 82
expertise, 27, 58, 123, 129
Fab Labs, 24–28
Facebook, 18, 68, 92, 93, 128, 135, 137
federated search, 87
fee
   registration, 16
   structure, 15

fines, 16
flexibility, 82
France, 4, 7–9, 11, 13, 16, 23, 25–27, 52, 69, 74, 93, 97, 99, 119, 122, 129, 139
free, 16, 19
   circulation of knowledge, 15
   information, 11, 17

G, H

geolocalization, 105, 106
Germany, 107
gold road, 99
Google, 17
governance
   corporate, 5
   information, 21
gray literature, 19, 88
Great Britain, 6
green road, 99
hackerspaces, 24, 25
Horizon 2020, 100
human
   and social sciences, 129
   dimension, 125

I

ideation, 69
identity, 131, 132, 137
   cultural, 132
   digital, 111, 128, 130, 131, 133, 135, 136
   social, 132
IFLA (International Federation of Library Associations), 8, 37
image, 12, 29, 33, 34, 72, 89, 91, 112, 115, 118, 122, 139, 143
   brand, 29, 112
   of libraries, 12, 122
immigration, 126
individualized services, 123

information, 3–7, 9–21, 23, 25,
  26, 29–31, 33–35, 37, 42, 43,
  49, 66, 68, 70, 71, 73–75,
  79–82, 85–91, 95, 97, 99, 100,
  103, 104, 106, 107, 111–117,
  119, 121–126, 128, 129, 133,
  134, 137, 139, 141, 142, 147
  devices, 124
  financial, 19
  flows, 114
  function, 10, 115
  literacy, 129
  market, 13
  paid, 17, 18
  providers, 11
  scientific and technical, 13
  technology, 79, 133
innovation(s), 3, 23, 24, 26, 34
inspiration, 69
Instagram, 86, 92–94, 128
intelligence, 18, 80, 88, 89, 103,
  106, 107
  artificial, 18, 106
  business, 88
interactions, 111
interlibrary loans, 103
internal communication support,
  117
Internet, 19
iteration, 69

J, L

Japan, 107
job(s), 13, 93
language lessons, 126
learning, 25, 28, 31, 68
  centers, 24, 28, 29
  deep, 107
lending automation, 107

LIBER (*Ligue des Bibliothèques
  Européennes de Recherche* –
  Association of European
  Research Libraries), 8
libraries, 9, 16, 94, 99, 106, 107,
  131
  digital, 85
  green, 37
  Intranets, 80, 85
  public, 12, 13, 15
  receptions, 124
  renovation, 56
  school, 129
  software, 88
  university, 13, 17, 32, 85, 129
LinkedIn, 93, 135
literature review, 129
logo, 34, 141, 143
loyalty, 72, 112

M

management, 3, 5, 21, 34, 38, 40,
  41, 43, 47–56, 58, 60, 63–66,
  69, 72, 75, 76, 82, 83, 85, 87,
  88, 104, 115–118, 121, 123,
  147, 148
  by benevolence, 47, 50
  by empathy, 47
  data, 104
  directive, 76
  library, 75
  of the user profile, 87
  participatory, 47, 76
  project(s), 47, 55
  theories, 47, 75
marketing, 4, 5, 14, 37, 67, 71,
  79, 90, 92, 111, 112, 114–116,
  118, 121, 122, 130, 131,
  139–143, 147, 148

digital, 90, 111, 131
library, 115, 116
techniques, 122
media, 140
mediation, 14, 26, 31, 76, 91, 99, 107
cultural, 127
digital, 127
information, 125
online, 87
pedagogical, 129
scientific, 128
social, 126
technological, 129
method(s)
agile, 66, 72–74
management, 66
of working, 68
scrum, 73
migrants, 37, 126
mission(s), 119
Mission Société Numérique, 25
monitoring, 13, 18, 91
information, 122
MOOC, 27
multimedia, 25

N, O

near-field communication, 106
need(s)
information, 33
of users, 121
Netherlands, 16
non-information professionals, 9
non-readers, 31
notoriety, 111
objects
augmented, 106
connected, 27
observation, 69

offer, 124
service(s), 79, 116, 123
online
purchases, 111
tutorials, 87
open, 11, 20, 25, 80, 95–100, 104, 129
access, 11, 95, 100
Archives Initiative (OAI), 97
archive(s), 15, 97, 99, 104
Data, 20, 25, 104, 129
opening hours, 9, 23, 36
organization
of work, 9, 107
thematic organization of resources, 122
outsourcing, 9

P, Q

PaaS (Platform as a Service), 81
part-time work, 6
partnerships, 34
patents, 19
patronage, 16, 140
pedagogy, 123
perception of the job, 7
Periscope, 129
personal assistance, 123
personnel, 48
photos, 94
Pinterest, 90–93
platform(s)
content curation, 91
digital, 80
archving of documents, 95
monitoring, 88
service, 86
library, 83
social, 91
podcasts, 129

policy
  communication, 92
  cultural, 127
  personal development, 48
  service(s), 80, 125
political decision-makers, 118
portals, 80, 85, 88
presence
  digital, 92
  online, 134
prisoners, 127
privatization of knowledge, 21
production
  of knowledge, 24, 30
  product approach, 34
products, 84
  information, 122
  library, 117
profession
  information–documentation, 6
project(s), 24, 115
  Adamant, 75
  corporate, 13
  digital, 73
  group, 59
  management, 60, 63
  marketing, 116
  service, 125
promotion, 115
protection, 39, 42, 104
  legal protection of individuals, 39
  of personal data, 42
prototypes, 67
public
  cultural action, 118
  reading, 12, 28, 126
publications, 10, 37, 88, 90, 96, 99, 100, 104, 129
  electronic, 96
  online, 129

publishers, 11, 71
Qatar, 24
QR codes, 105, 106
quality of service, 9

R, S

Radio Frequency Identification (RFID), 106
reports, 129
reader, 16
reality
  augmented, 104
  virtual, 106
reception, 33
recognition, 114
  facial, 11
  vocal, 11
recommendations, 70, 112, 113
referencing, 111
relationship, 6, 11, 29, 40, 72, 73, 92, 99, 127, 147
  of trust, 51
  service, 80, 124, 127, 128
remote working, 6, 27
reputation, 92, 135, 140, 142
  online, 111
research
  market, 116
researcher(s), 71, 129
resources
  documentary, 126
  human, 45
right, 88
robot(s), 107
robotization, 106
satisfaction, 142
school libraries, 129
scientific periodicals, 17
search engines, 18, 112, 114, 135

sector
  private, 12
  public, 12
serendipity, 142
service(s), 14, 79, 80, 122
  digital, 80, 86
  documentation, 9, 12, 13, 15, 18, 34
  individualized, 6
  library, 122
  obligation, 79
  one-off, 6
  private documentation, 15
  production management, 65
  public, 12, 16, 73, 79
  question and answer, 128, 141
  reference, 124
    virtual, 112
servuction, 14, 80
signage, 61
Singapore, 107
site web, 111
skills, 123
Slack, 81
slogan, 34, 71, 141
Smart Libraries, 29–31
Snapchat, 94
social
  cohesion, 127
  link, 23
  networks, 39, 88, 91, 128, 133, 136
space(s), 27
  digital public, 26
  learning, 29
  library, 23, 24, 35
  social, 127
  work, 59
standards, 14, 19
storage of documents, 42
streaming, 20

students, 32, 36
subscriptions to journals, 10
subsidarity, 48
survey(s), 116
  satisfaction, 122
Swiss Library Service Platform, 11, 84, 85
Switzerland, 17, 35, 98
system(s)
  integrated library management, 40, 41
  recommendation, 71, 88
  value, 139

T, U

teacher-documentalists, 129
technicality, 123
thematic hub, 123
theory of knowledge commons, 20
third place, 24
traces, 135, 136
training
  continuous training of personnel, 5
  for the public, 124
  of users, 122
trust, 65, 76
Tumblr, 94
Twitter, 81, 92, 93, 128, 129, 135
United States, 16, 28, 37, 94
universities, 16
use, 23
user(s), 15, 18, 33, 69, 71, 79, 122
  approach, 34
  experience, 47, 66, 69, 142

V, W, Y

value-added tax, 11
video(s), 20, 93, 95
virtual exhibitions, 119

visibility, 79
vision, 54, 85, 96, 118, 119, 121, 122
visual component, 87
volunteering, 12
walking reference, 121
well-treatment, 50
wellness, 31
Wikipedia, 20
working practices, 74
world
   of professional associations, 7
   working, 4, 24
WorldShare, 83
worldwide summit on the information society, 17
young
   adults, 32
   audience, 32
YouTube, 86, 92–95, 129

Other titles from

in

Information Systems, Web and Pervasive Computing

2022

BRÉZILLON Patrick, TURNER Roy M.
Modeling and Use of Context in Action

KARAM Elie
General Contractor Business Model for Smart Cities: Fundamentals and Techniques

2021

BEN REBAH Hassen, BOUKTHIR Hafedh, CHÉDEBOIS Antoine
Website Design and Development with HTML5 and CSS3

EL ASSAD Safwan, BARBA Dominique
Digital Communications 1: Fundamentals and Techniques
Digital Communications 2: Directed and Practical Work

GAUDIN Thierry, MAUREL Marie-Christine, POMEROL Jean-Charles
Chance, Calculation and Life

LAURENT Sébastien-Yves
Conflicts, Crimes and Regulations in Cyberspace
(Cybersecurity Set – Volume 2)

LE DEUFF Olivier
Hyperdocumentation (Intellectual Technologies Set – Volume 9)

PÉLISSIER Maud
Cultural Commons in the Digital Ecosystem
(Intellectual Technologies Set – Volume 8)

2020

CLIQUET Gérard, with the collaboration of BARAY Jérôme
Location-Based Marketing: Geomarketing and Geolocation

DE FRÉMINVILLE Marie
Cybersecurity and Decision Makers: Data Security and Digital Trust

GEORGE Éric
Digitalization of Society and Socio-political Issues 2: Digital, Information and Research

HELALI Saida
Systems and Network Infrastructure Integration

LOISEAU Hugo, VENTRE Daniel, ADEN Hartmut
Cybersecurity in Humanities and Social Sciences: A Research Methods Approach (Cybersecurity Set – Volume 1)

SEDKAOUI Soraya, KHELFAOUI Mounia
Sharing Economy and Big Data Analytics

SCHMITT Églantine
Big Data: An Art of Decision Making
(Intellectual Technologies Set – Volume 7)

2019

ALBAN Daniel, EYNAUD Philippe, MALAURENT Julien, RICHET Jean-Loup, VITARI Claudio
Information Systems Management: Governance, Urbanization and Alignment

AUGEY Dominique, with the collaboration of ALCARAZ Marina
Digital Information Ecosystems: Smart Press

BATTON-HUBERT Mireille, DESJARDIN Eric, PINET François
Geographic Data Imperfection 1: From Theory to Applications

BRIQUET-DUHAZÉ Sophie, TURCOTTE Catherine
From Reading-Writing Research to Practice

BROCHARD Luigi, KAMATH Vinod, CORBALAN Julita, HOLLAND Scott, MITTELBACH Walter, OTT Michael
Energy-Efficient Computing and Data Centers

CHAMOUX Jean-Pierre
The Digital Era 2: Political Economy Revisited

COCHARD Gérard-Michel
Introduction to Stochastic Processes and Simulation

DUONG Véronique
SEO Management: Methods and Techniques to Achieve Success

GAUCHEREL Cédric, GOUYON Pierre-Henri, DESSALLES Jean-Louis
Information, The Hidden Side of Life

GEORGE Éric
Digitalization of Society and Socio-political Issues 1: Digital, Communication and Culture

GHLALA Riadh
Analytic SQL in SQL Server 2014/2016

JANIER Mathilde, SAINT-DIZIER Patrick
Argument Mining: Linguistic Foundations

SOURIS Marc
Epidemiology and Geography: Principles, Methods and Tools of Spatial Analysis

TOUNSI Wiem
Cyber-Vigilance and Digital Trust: Cyber Security in the Era of Cloud Computing and IoT

2018

ARDUIN Pierre-Emmanuel
Insider Threats
(Advances in Information Systems Set – Volume 10)

CARMÈS Maryse
Digital Organizations Manufacturing: Scripts, Performativity and Semiopolitics
(Intellectual Technologies Set – Volume 5)

CARRÉ Dominique, VIDAL Geneviève
Hyperconnectivity: Economical, Social and Environmental Challenges
(Computing and Connected Society Set – Volume 3)

CHAMOUX Jean-Pierre
The Digital Era 1: Big Data Stakes

DOUAY Nicolas
Urban Planning in the Digital Age
(Intellectual Technologies Set – Volume 6)

FABRE Renaud, BENSOUSSAN Alain
The Digital Factory for Knowledge: Production and Validation of Scientific Results

GAUDIN Thierry, LACROIX Dominique, MAUREL Marie-Christine, POMEROL Jean-Charles
Life Sciences, Information Sciences

GAYARD Laurent
Darknet: Geopolitics and Uses
(Computing and Connected Society Set – Volume 2)

IAFRATE Fernando
Artificial Intelligence and Big Data: The Birth of a New Intelligence
(Advances in Information Systems Set – Volume 8)

LE DEUFF Olivier
Digital Humanities: History and Development
(Intellectual Technologies Set – Volume 4)

MANDRAN Nadine
Traceable Human Experiment Design Research: Theoretical Model and Practical Guide
(Advances in Information Systems Set – Volume 9)

PIVERT Olivier
NoSQL Data Models: Trends and Challenges

ROCHET Claude
Smart Cities: Reality or Fiction

SALEH Imad, AMMI, Mehdi, SZONIECKY Samuel
Challenges of the Internet of Things: Technology, Use, Ethics
(Digital Tools and Uses Set – Volume 7)

SAUVAGNARGUES Sophie
Decision-making in Crisis Situations: Research and Innovation for Optimal Training

SEDKAOUI Soraya
Data Analytics and Big Data

SZONIECKY Samuel
Ecosystems Knowledge: Modeling and Analysis Method for Information and Communication
(Digital Tools and Uses Set – Volume 6)

2017

BOUHAÏ Nasreddine, SALEH Imad
Internet of Things: Evolutions and Innovations
(Digital Tools and Uses Set – Volume 4)

DUONG Véronique
Baidu SEO: Challenges and Intricacies of Marketing in China

LESAS Anne-Marie, MIRANDA Serge
The Art and Science of NFC Programming
(Intellectual Technologies Set – Volume 3)

LIEM André
Prospective Ergonomics
(Human-Machine Interaction Set – Volume 4)

MARSAULT Xavier
Eco-generative Design for Early Stages of Architecture
(Architecture and Computer Science Set – Volume 1)

REYES-GARCIA Everardo
The Image-Interface: Graphical Supports for Visual Information
(Digital Tools and Uses Set – Volume 3)

REYES-GARCIA Everardo, BOUHAÏ Nasreddine
Designing Interactive Hypermedia Systems
(Digital Tools and Uses Set – Volume 2)

SAÏD Karim, BAHRI KORBI Fadia
Asymmetric Alliances and Information Systems:Issues and Prospects
(Advances in Information Systems Set – Volume 7)

SZONIECKY Samuel, BOUHAÏ Nasreddine
Collective Intelligence and Digital Archives: Towards Knowledge Ecosystems
(Digital Tools and Uses Set – Volume 1)

2016

BEN CHOUIKHA Mona
Organizational Design for Knowledge Management

BERTOLO David
Interactions on Digital Tablets in the Context of 3D Geometry Learning
(Human-Machine Interaction Set – Volume 2)

BOUVARD Patricia, SUZANNE Hervé
Collective Intelligence Development in Business

EL FALLAH SEGHROUCHNI Amal, ISHIKAWA Fuyuki, HÉRAULT Laurent, TOKUDA Hideyuki
Enablers for Smart Cities

FABRE Renaud, in collaboration with MESSERSCHMIDT-MARIET Quentin, HOLVOET Margot
New Challenges for Knowledge

GAUDIELLO Ilaria, ZIBETTI Elisabetta
Learning Robotics, with Robotics, by Robotics
(Human–Machine Interaction Set – Volume 3)

HENROTIN Joseph
The Art of War in the Network Age
(Intellectual Technologies Set – Volume 1)

KITAJIMA Munéo
Memory and Action Selection in Human–Machine Interaction
(Human–Machine Interaction Set – Volume 1)

LAGRAÑA Fernando
E-mail and Behavioral Changes: Uses and Misuses of Electronic Communications

LEIGNEL Jean-Louis, UNGARO Thierry, STAAR Adrien
Digital Transformation
(Advances in Information Systems Set – Volume 6)

NOYER Jean-Max
Transformation of Collective Intelligences
(Intellectual Technologies Set – Volume 2)

VENTRE Daniel
Information Warfare – 2nd edition

VITALIS André
The Uncertain Digital Revolution
(Computing and Connected Society Set – Volume 1)

2015

ARDUIN Pierre-Emmanuel, GRUNDSTEIN Michel, ROSENTHAL-SABROUX Camille
Information and Knowledge System
(Advances in Information Systems Set – Volume 2)

BÉRANGER Jérôme
Medical Information Systems Ethics

BRONNER Gérald
Belief and Misbelief Asymmetry on the Internet

IAFRATE Fernando
From Big Data to Smart Data
(Advances in Information Systems Set – Volume 1)

KRICHEN Saoussen, BEN JOUIDA Sihem
Supply Chain Management and its Applications in Computer Science

NEGRE Elsa
Information and Recommender Systems
(Advances in Information Systems Set – Volume 4)

POMEROL Jean-Charles, EPELBOIN Yves, THOURY Claire
MOOCs

SALLES Maryse
Decision-Making and the Information System
(Advances in Information Systems Set – Volume 3)

SAMARA Tarek
ERP and Information Systems: Integration or Disintegration
(Advances in Information Systems Set – Volume 5)

2014

DINET Jérôme
Information Retrieval in Digital Environments

HÉNO Raphaële, CHANDELIER Laure
3D Modeling of Buildings: Outstanding Sites

KEMBELLEC Gérald, CHARTRON Ghislaine, SALEH Imad
Recommender Systems

MATHIAN Hélène, SANDERS Lena
Spatio-temporal Approaches: Geographic Objects and Change Process

PLANTIN Jean-Christophe
Participatory Mapping

VENTRE Daniel
Chinese Cybersecurity and Defense

2013

BERNIK Igor
Cybercrime and Cyberwarfare

CAPET Philippe, DELAVALLADE Thomas
Information Evaluation

LEBRATY Jean-Fabrice, LOBRE-LEBRATY Katia
Crowdsourcing: One Step Beyond

SALLABERRY Christian
Geographical Information Retrieval in Textual Corpora

2012

BUCHER Bénédicte, LE BER Florence
Innovative Software Development in GIS

GAUSSIER Eric, YVON François
Textual Information Access

STOCKINGER Peter
Audiovisual Archives: Digital Text and Discourse Analysis

VENTRE Daniel
Cyber Conflict

2011

BANOS Arnaud, THÉVENIN Thomas
Geographical Information and Urban Transport Systems

DAUPHINÉ André
Fractal Geography

LEMBERGER Pirmin, MOREL Mederic
Managing Complexity of Information Systems

STOCKINGER Peter
Introduction to Audiovisual Archives

STOCKINGER Peter
Digital Audiovisual Archives

VENTRE Daniel
Cyberwar and Information Warfare

2010

BONNET Pierre
Enterprise Data Governance

BRUNET Roger
Sustainable Geography

CARREGA Pierre
Geographical Information and Climatology

CAUVIN Colette, ESCOBAR Francisco, SERRADJ Aziz
Thematic Cartography – 3-volume series
Thematic Cartography and Transformations – Volume 1
Cartography and the Impact of the Quantitative Revolution – Volume 2
New Approaches in Thematic Cartography – Volume 3

LANGLOIS Patrice
Simulation of Complex Systems in GIS

MATHIS Philippe
Graphs and Networks – 2nd edition

THERIAULT Marius, DES ROSIERS François
Modeling Urban Dynamics

2009

BONNET Pierre, DETAVERNIER Jean-Michel, VAUQUIER Dominique
Sustainable IT Architecture: the Progressive Way of Overhauling Information Systems with SOA

PAPY Fabrice
Information Science

RIVARD François, ABOU HARB Georges, MERET Philippe
The Transverse Information System

ROCHE Stéphane, CARON Claude
Organizational Facets of GIS

2008

BRUGNOT Gérard
Spatial Management of Risks

FINKE Gerd
Operations Research and Networks

GUERMOND Yves
Modeling Process in Geography

KANEVSKI Michael
Advanced Mapping of Environmental Data

MANOUVRIER Bernard, LAURENT Ménard
Application Integration: EAI, B2B, BPM and SOA

PAPY Fabrice
Digital Libraries

2007

DOBESCH Hartwig, DUMOLARD Pierre, DYRAS Izabela
Spatial Interpolation for Climate Data

SANDERS Lena
Models in Spatial Analysis

2006

CLIQUET Gérard
Geomarketing

CORNIOU Jean-Pierre
Looking Back and Going Forward in IT

DEVILLERS Rodolphe, JEANSOULIN Robert
Fundamentals of Spatial Data Quality

Printed and bound by CPI Group (UK) Ltd, Croydon, CR0 4YY
21/11/2022

03164994-0001